Greening Industry:
New Roles for Communities, Markets, and Governments

A World Bank Policy Research Report

Greening Industry:
New Roles for Communities, Markets, and Governments

Published for the World Bank
Oxford University Press

DELHI   BOMBAY CALCUTTA   MADRAS   KARACHI
KUALA LUMPUR   SINGAPORE   HONG KONG   TOKYO
NAIROBI   DAR ES SALAAM   CAPE TOWN
MELBOURNE   AUCKLAND

and associated companies in

BERLIN   IBADAN

© 2000 The International Bank for Reconstruction
and Development / The World Bank
1818 H Street, N.W.,
Washington, D.C. 20433

Published by Oxford University Press, Inc.
198 Madison Avenue, New York, N.Y. 10016

Manufactured in the United States of America
First printing October 1999

Cover credits: front cover, Tantyo Bangun-Indo Pix; back cover, from top to bottom,
Curt Carnemark/World Bank, Curt Carnemark/World Bank, Corbis

The boundaries, colors, denominations, and other information shown on the maps in
this volume do not imply on the part of the World Bank Group any judgment on the
legal status of any territory or the endorsement or acceptance of such boundaries.

Library of Congress Cataloging-in-Publication (CIP) Data.

Greening industry : new roles for communities, markets, and governments /
    Development Research Group, World Bank.
        p.   cm.
    Includes bibliographical references.
    ISBN 0-19-521127-8
    1. Pollution—Developing countries.   2. Environmental policy—Developing
countries.   3. Sustainable development.   I. World Bank.
Development Research Group.
HC59.72.P55G74   1999
333.7—dc21
                                                    99-15989
                                                      CIP

This book was printed using recycled paper and soy based ink.
The cover stock is 12pt. Cornwall, 15% post consumer waste.
The cd sleeve is 10pt. Cornwall, 15% post consumer waste.
The text stock is 70 # Mohawk 50% recycled, with 15% post consumer waste.

Table of Contents

Text Figures

Tables

Foreword

Over one hundred developing countries have joined the United Nations since Japan's Minamata disaster in 1956. Almost all have environmental agencies, in part because Japan's tragic encounter with heavy-metal poisoning helped spark an international effort to control industrial pollution. The first phase of this effort culminated in 1972, when the United Nations established its Environment Programme and the international community convened the Stockholm Conference on Sustainable Development. Between Stockholm and the Rio Earth Summit in 1992, most developing countries set up institutions to regulate pollution. They made steady progress, although it was usually eclipsed by media coverage of disasters such as the lethal landslides in Cubatao, Brazil, and the pesticide factory explosion in Bhopal, India, which killed and injured thousands.

Still, pollution regulation arrived in the developing world as an import. Instead of creating new approaches from scratch, most agencies adopted traditional command-and-control regulation with technical assistance from the OECD countries. Unfortunately, this particular import didn't always adapt well to local conditions. By the early 1990s, regulators in many countries had concluded that conventional methods were too expensive and often ineffective. Innovators began experimenting with new approaches, and some yielded excellent results. At the same time, many national economic reforms were proving to be effective in fighting pollution.

In this report, we show why these macro and regulatory policy reforms are defining a new model for pollution control in developing countries. We write as participant-observers, because we have helped establish programs as well as studied their impact. Since 1993, we have been privileged to collaborate with pioneers of the new approach in Jakarta, Bogota, Beijing, Rio, Manila, Mexico City,

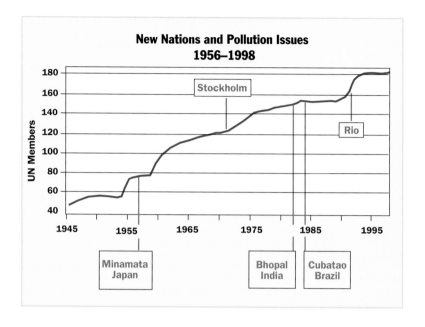

and elsewhere. This report is really their story. It is also the story of our colleagues in the World Bank and other international agencies. Behind the scenes, they have worked tirelessly to provide new environmental agencies with financial support, technical assistance, and information about the progress of reform in other countries.

The news we bring is hopeful. After six years of research, policy experimentation, and firsthand observation, we believe that environmentally sustainable industrial development is within reach. Greening industry will take time, but even the poorest countries can accomplish it. In this report we show why, and suggest strategies for moving forward.

The Report Team

The principal author of **Greening Industry: New Roles for Communities, Markets, and Governments** is David Wheeler, Lead Economist for the Infrastructure/Environment Team of the World Bank's Development Research Group. **Greening Industry** summarizes six years of research and project work by a core team of economists, environmental engineers, and policy analysts: Shakeb Afsah, Susmita Dasgupta, David Gray, Raymond Hartman, Hemamala Hettige, Mainul Huq, Benoit Laplante, Robert Lucas, Nlandu Mamingi, Muthukumara Mani, Paul Martin, Craig Meisner, Sheoli Pargal, David Shaman, Manjula Singh, Hua Wang, David Witzel and Ping Yun. The report was produced under the direction of Joseph Stiglitz, Lyn Squire, Paul Collier, and Zmarak Shalizi.

To learn more about the World Bank's research in this area, please visit the **New Ideas in Pollution Regulation** website at **http://www.worldbank.org/nipr**. Material from this website is also included on the CD-ROM that accompanies **Greening Industry**.

Acknowledgments

This report is the product of an extensive research effort by the World Bank's Development Economics Vice Presidency. The cornerstone of our research strategy has been a program of collaboration with developing-country environmental agencies in the design, implementation and evaluation of new approaches to pollution control. As participant-observers, we have learned a tremendous amount from the pioneers who are showing how innovative programs can reduce pollution significantly, even in very poor countries. We are particularly indebted to the following colleagues:

Brazil—from the Environmental Protection Agency for Rio de Janeiro State, FEEMA: Sergio Margulis, former President, Paulo de Gusmao, former Director for Environmental Planning, and Joao Batista; from the Brazilian Institute for Geography and Statistics, IBGE: José Enílcio Rocha Collares, Chief of DERNA, Patrícia Portella Ferreira Alves, Chief of DIEAM, Eloísa Domingues, ISTAM Project Manager, Rosane de Andrade Memoria Moreno and Lucy Teixeira Guimarães, Technical Team, Industrial Pollution Project; from the Environmental Protection Agency for Sao Paulo State, CETESB: Luis Carlos da Costa.

China—from the State Environmental Protection Agency, SEPA: Kunmin Zhang, Deputy Administrator, Xiaomin Guo, Fengzhong Cao and Qingfeng Zhang; from the Chinese Research Academy of Environmental Sciences, CRAES: Jinnan Wang and Dong Cao; from Nanjing University: Genfa Lu.

Colombia—from the Ministry of the Environment, Office of Economic Analysis: Thomas Black Arbelaez, Director, Martha Patricia Castillo, Ana Maria Diaz-Ciceres and Maria Claudia Garcia; from the pollution control agency for Oriente Antioqueno, CORNARE: Leonardo Munoz Cardona, Director and Luis Fernando Castro, Pollution Control Director.

India—from the Central Pollution Control Board: Dilip Biswas, Chairman; from the Environmental Protection Training and Research Institute: C. Uma Maheswari, Joint Director; from the Andrah Pradesh Pollution Control Board: Tishya Chatterjee.

Indonesia—Sarwono Kusumaatmadja, former State Minister of Environment; from Indonesia's Environmental Impact Management Agency, BAPEDAL: Nabiel Makarim, former Deputy for Pollution Control, Made Setiawan and Dama Ratunanda.

Mexico—from the Secretariat for Environment, Natural Resources and Fisheries, SEMARNAP; National Institute for Ecology, INE: Francisco Giner de los Ríos, General Director for Environmental Regulation, Adrián Fernández Bremauntz, Director General for Environmental Management and Information, Luis R. Sánchez Cataño, Director for Metropolitan Environmental Management, and Luis F. Guadarrama.

Philippines—from the Department of Environment and Natural Resources, DENR: former Minister Victor Ramos and Bebet Gozun; from the University of the Philippines: Tonet Tanchuling and Alex Casilla.

We are indebted to many colleagues in the World Bank who have directly supported our work and/or participated in our collaborative program: Kulsum Ahmed, Adriana Bianchi, Dan Biller, Carter Brandon, Richard Calkins, Cecilia Guido-Spano, Ken Chomitz, Maureen Cropper, Shelton Davis, Adrian Demayo, Michelle De Nevers, Charles DiLeva, Yasmin D'Souza, Evelyn de Castro, Clara Else, Gunnar Eskeland, Ben Fisher, Kristalina Georgieva, David Hanrahan, Patrice Harou, Nicholas Hope, Patchamuthu Illangovan, Gregory Ingram, Maritta Koch-Weser, Vijay Jagannathan, Emmanuel Jimenez, Todd Johnson, Andres Liebenthal, Lawrence MacDonald, Anna Maranon, Richard Newfarmer, Saed Ordoubadi, Mead Over, Jan Post, Violetta Rosenthal, Elizabeth Schaper, Teresa Serra, Katherine Sierra, Lyn Squire, Andrew Steer, Laura Tlaiye, Lee Travers, Walter Vergara, Joachim Von Amsberg, Konrad Von Ritter, Thomas Walton and Roula Yazigi.

We would also like to thank the following World Bank colleagues for their assistance, advice, and insights: Richard Ackermann, Jean Aden, Nick Anderson, Bernard Baratz, Carl Bartone, Roger Batstone, Antonio Bento, Jan Bojo, Annice Brown, Shantayanan Devarajan, John Dixon, David Dollar, Alfred Duda, Jack Fritz, Richard Gains, Robert Goodland, Daniel Gross, Kirk Hamilton, Jeffrey Hammer, Nagaraja Rao Harshadeep, Gordon Hughes, Frannie Humplick, Ian Johnson, Bjorn Larsen, Stephen Lintner, Magda Lovei, Kseniya Lvovsky, Dennis Mahar, Desmond McCarthy, Jean-Roger Mercier, Ashoka Mody, Carl-Heinz Mumme, Lant Pritchett, Ramesh Ramankutty, Geoffrey Read, John Redwood, Jitendra Shah, Sudhir Shetty, Karlis Smits, Sari Soderstrom, John Williamson, Jian Xie and C.H. Zhang.

Book design, editing, and production were directed and managed by the Production Services Unit of the World Bank's Office of the Publisher. Sandra Hackman played a major role in editing the report. David Shaman coordinated production of the report for the Bank's Development Research Group.

Greening Industry: New Roles for Communities, Markets, and Governments

C onventional wisdom holds that developing countries cannot hope to clean up industrial pollution of their air and water until they reach a level of affluence seen today only in wealthy countries. According to this view, continued expansion of industrial output will inevitably worsen the already severe levels of pollution that are common today in urban areas of the developing world. Another prevalent belief is that growing global trade and open borders are encouraging dirty industries to move to developing countries, which cannot afford to curb environmental abuses.

Six years of research, policy experiments, and firsthand observation have shown this picture to be false. Factories in many poor countries run cleaner than a decade ago, and total emissions are actually falling in some areas where industry is growing rapidly. What's more, "pollution havens"—developing countries that provide a permanent home to dirty industries—have failed to materialize. Instead, poorer nations and communities are acting to reduce pollution because they have decided that the benefits of abatement outweigh the costs.

Environmental regulators in developing countries are trying fresh approaches and finding new allies in the battle to curb pollution. These initiatives stem from widespread recognition that traditional pollution regulation is inappropriate for many developing countries. New regulatory institutions are often unable to enforce conventional discharge standards at the factory level. Many regulators also recognize that such standards are not cost-effective because they require all polluting factories to toe the same line, regardless of abatement costs and local environmental conditions.

To break out of this one-size-fits-all approach, developing-country regulators are opting for more flexible and efficient systems that nevertheless provide strong incentives for polluters to clean up. Some of the pioneers have turned to financial incentives by charging polluters for every unit of their emissions. As results from programs in Colombia, China, and Philippines have shown, many managers opt for serious pollution control when they face steep, regular payments for emissions. And pollution charges not only cut emissions but generate public revenue as well—which in turn can support local efforts to control pollution.

Other environmental reformers are using simple rating systems to publicly recognize factories that adhere to local and national pollution standards—and to train the communal eye on those that do not. By classifying factories based on their reported emissions, and widely broadcasting the results, regulators are enabling communities to identify serious polluters and pressure them to clean up. This channel for "informal" regulation has proven to be potent, even in cases where formal regulation is weak or absent. Such public disclosure programs also enlist the efforts of investors, lenders, and consumers, whose concern over liability from poor environmental practices and desire to reward green manufacturers brings pressure to bear on polluters. Indonesia and Philippines, in particular, have shown that such public disclosure programs can curb pollution at modest cost.

Public education regarding the sources and impacts of pollution also provides a powerful lever for improving the lives of poor people, who suffer greatly from emissions even as industry's pollution intensity declines. Armed with good information, poor citizens can work with environmental agencies and elect political leaders willing to pressure factories to curb emissions, as regions and countries make the transition to greener industry.

To ensure the success of such programs, regulators are relying on low-cost computer technology that cuts the cost of gathering, processing, and distributing information. Selective, focused use of environmental databases and computer models, along with public involvement, also helps communities and businesses negotiate environmental priorities and action plans based on a common understanding of the impact of pollution and the cost of abating it.

These initiatives are working because they have a solid economic foundation. Plant managers do not pollute because they enjoy fouling the air and water but because they are trying to minimize their costs, so they will tolerate emissions up to the point where the penalty for more pollution becomes greater than the cost of controlling it. In fact, managers' sensitivity to costs gives regulators many opportunities to influence their decisions. At the factory level, for example, environmental agencies can lower pollution-control costs by supporting training in environmental management for small and medium-scale enterprises. Recent pilot projects in Mexico have shown that such programs can provide a cost-effective complement to conventional regulation.

At the national level, economic reforms can also reduce pollution. Greater openness to trade can enhance managers' access to cleaner technology, while cutting subsidies for raw materials can encourage companies to reduce waste. State-owned enterprises are often heavy polluters, so privatization can contribute to cleaner production. Countries as diverse as China, India, and Brazil have demonstrated the power of such measures to reduce pollution. But economic reforms are no panacea, because growth-promoting measures can make local pollution worse in some cases. To ensure sustainable development, economic reformers should anticipate such impacts and work closely with environmental agencies to offset them.

Overall, the proliferation of innovative channels for reducing emissions has created a new model for pollution control in developing countries. In this model, regulation is information intensive and transparent. As environmental agencies exert influence through formal and informal channels, they become more like mediators and less like dictators. Community representatives take their place at the negotiating table along with regulators and factory managers. Market agents make their presence felt through the decisions of consumers, bankers, and stockholders.

The new model gives policymakers more options, but it also imposes new responsibilities—for strategic thinking about the benefits and costs of pollution control; a strong commitment to public participation; clever, focused use of information technologies; and willingness to try new approaches such as pollution charges and public disclosure. Of course, regulators will always have important responsibilities for monitoring factories' environmental performance and enforcing regulations. But in the new model, regulators use more resources to provide better public information, encourage informal regulation, furnish technical assistance to managers, and promote environmentally sound economic reforms.

We write about this model as participant-observers, because we have helped establish many of the innovative programs that we discuss, as well as studied their impact. Since 1993, we have collaborated with pioneers of the new model in Indonesia, Colombia, China, Brazil, Philippines, Mexico, and other countries. This report is really the story of those pioneers—their ideas, programs, and results. It is also the story of our colleagues in the World Bank and other international agencies who have worked tirelessly to provide the reformers with financial support, technical assistance, and information about environmental initiatives in other countries.

Together, these experiences have persuaded us that the conventional wisdom is wrong: Economic development and industrial pollution are not immutably linked. We are convinced that developing countries can build on the new model to reduce industrial pollution significantly, even if they grow rapidly during the coming decade.

Chongqing, 1998

Source: *Katrinka Ebbe*

Chapter One

Is Industrial Pollution the Price of Development?

In China, a generation of economic growth has given millions a lifestyle beyond the dreams of their grandparents. China's urban consumers celebrate their new prosperity by strolling through downtown malls in cities like Chongqing. But as China's cities have boomed, the simple pleasures of sunshine and clear air have been lost. Pollution from motor vehicles, smokestacks, and home hearths is so thick that Chongqing consumers can't see the tops of office towers a few blocks away. The most dangerous pollutants are particulates—tiny airborne particles that lodge deep in the lungs, causing severe and sometimes fatal respiratory problems. In four Chinese cities alone—Chongqing, Beijing, Shanghai, and Shenyang—10,000 people will die prematurely this year from exposure to particulates.

In the filthy clouds hanging over China's cities and the smog plaguing other poor countries, unspoken questions lurk: Is pollution simply the price of development? Does this generation have to endure an environmental tragedy for the sake of future generations? Many people in both developed and developing countries believe the answer is yes, as stories in the popular media often reinforce the idea that pollution control is limited to the industrial economies. After all, the proof is right before our eyes . . . or is it?

In fact, recent evidence shows that many developing countries have already turned the corner in the fight against industrial pollution. Factories are running cleaner than a decade ago, and total emissions are starting to fall even in areas where industry continues to grow rapidly. The cleanup has begun because developing countries have decided that the benefits of pollution control outweigh the costs.

This realization has prompted many countries to adopt innovative strategies that enlist local communities, consumers, investors, and economic policy reformers in the struggle against industrial pollution. Polluters, in turn, are discovering that they have no place to hide—and showing that they can reduce pollution quickly while producing profitably if regulators provide the right incentives. Industrial pollution is still exacting a heavy price in developing countries, but there is no longer any reason to accept it as the price of development.

1.1 Kuznets Revisited

A generation ago, the U.S. economist Simon Kuznets proposed that income inequality generally rises as development proceeds, falling only after the rewards of growth accumulate. Similarly, some researchers have claimed to identify an environmental Kuznets curve, in which pollution from industry, motor vehicles, and households increases until development generates enough wealth to promote significant pollution control. Whether the turning point occurs when countries reach per capita incomes of $5,000 or $15,000 per year has never been clear. But the implication is that for highly polluted cities in poor countries (Figure 1.1), another generation of growth will create nightmarish conditions.

Fortunately, the evidence doesn't support such a bleak vision. São Paulo, for example, has lower particulate air pollution than Los Angeles (Figure 1.1), and Bombay's level is scarcely higher. Present-day Jakarta and Santiago have air quality comparable to that of many developed-country cities in the 1950s—yet the former have much lower incomes.

China's growth experience casts further doubt on the environmental Kuznets curve, which would predict rapidly increasing pollution in such a poor country. Recent data suggest that average urban air quality in that country has stabilized or improved since the mid-1980s (Fig. 1.2).

At best, environmental Kuznets curves provide snapshots of a dynamic relationship between pollution and development that is evolving in response to experience. To understand the forces underlying this evolution, we need to pay closer attention to the complex factors driving environmental progress in developing countries.

Figure 1.1   Air Pollution In World Megacities

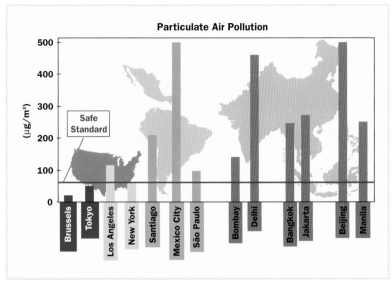

Source: UNEP/WHO, 1992

Figure 1.2   Air Pollution in Urban China, 1987–1995

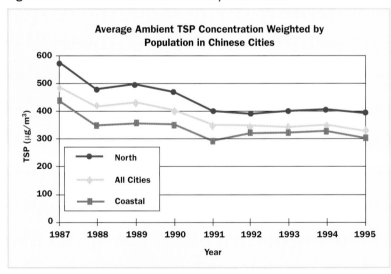

Source: China Environmental Yearbooks (SEPA)

1.2 Focusing on Pollution from Industry

In many cities, a large share of air pollution comes from motor vehicles and home hearths, while household sewage is a major contributor to water pollution. Emissions from industry are also pervasive, although they vary considerably in relative importance. At one extreme, China's State Environmental Protection Agency estimates that pollution from factories accounts for over 70 percent of the national total, including 70 percent of organic water pollution, 72 percent of sulfur dioxide emissions, and 75 percent of flue dust, a major component of suspended particulates. Many polluting industries are located in China's densely populated metropolitan areas, where emissions exposure can cause particularly serious damage to human health and economic activity.

In many Brazilian cities, by contrast, households and motor vehicles emit the lion's share of serious air and water pollution. These major pollution sources deserve serious attention. However, this report will focus on emissions from factories rather than attempting a comprehensive analysis of urban pollution. We have chosen to work on emissions from industry for two main reasons besides their significant contribution to overall pollution. First, we are following the lead of our colleagues in developing-country environmental agencies. During their first phase of development, they have focused their limited resources on major industrial polluters. Such polluters are feasible to regulate because they are stationary, relatively easy to identify, and more amenable to pollution control than smaller polluters such as households, informal-sector enterprises, and motor vehicles.

Emissions from industry also provide an excellent domain for comparative analysis because they are more highly varied than those from other sources. Industry emits hundreds of air, water, and solid pollutants, contributing to smog, buildup of heavy metals, organic water pollution, hazardous solid waste, and many other sources of damage to communities and ecosystems. Investigating these highly varied emissions has generated a wealth of new information for sound environmental policy making: on the sources of pollution, their relative contributions to environmental damage, and differences in the costs of controlling them.

Rather than providing an exhaustive treatment of the issues surrounding control of industrial pollution, we highlight recent experiences with regulatory and economic policy reforms whose impacts have been documented. Rich sources of complementary social and economic data from standard national surveys facilitate this study.

Equipped with such data, we have been able to investigate the role of many factors in promoting pollution reduction.

1.3 How Economic Development Affects Pollution and Regulation

Because regulatory institutions in many poor countries are weak, we might expect factories to pollute with no restraint. However, consider the record of three Asian developing countries: Bangladesh, Indonesia, and Philippines. The poorest is Bangladesh: In a flood- and cyclone-prone area the size of an average U.S. state, 115 million Bangladeshis subsist on an average income of US$270 per year. The country is just beginning to regulate pollution, and industrial sectors such as paper, chemicals, and fertilizer nearly always discharge wastes into rivers that serve downstream populations. However, a study of fertilizer plants in Bangladesh finds wide variation in their environmental performance. Some are serious polluters, while others have made major efforts to control their emissions (Box 1.1).

Traditionally, Indonesia and Philippines have also lacked a strong commitment to enforcing pollution control regulations. During the past few years, however, both countries have begun programs for rating and publicly disclosing factories' compliance with regulations (see Chapter 3). The programs have rated several hundred factories for over two years, and at least half now adhere to organic water pollution regulations in each country (Figure 1.3).[1]

Figure 1.3 Polluting Factories in Philippines and Indonesia

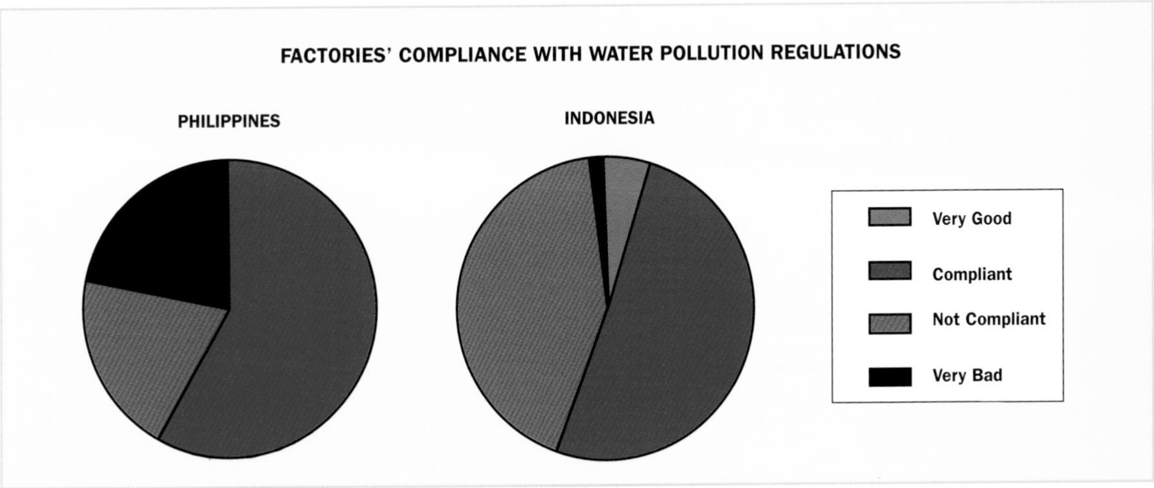

Sources: DENR (Philippines); BAPEDAL (Indonesia)

Box 1.1   Four Fertilizer Plants in Bangladesh

In 1992, a World Bank team surveyed four of the five urea fertilizer plants in Bangladesh (Huq and Wheeler, 1992). All of these plants were public enterprises managed by the Bangladesh Chemical Industries Corp. (BCIC), but their ages varied widely, and they were scattered in urban and rural locations throughout the country. All the plants were located on rivers into which they discharged their wastewater. All used natural gas as the basic feedstock, included both ammonia and urea facilities, and operated on self-generated electricity.

Our survey investigated process technologies, end-of-pipe treatment efforts, and the efficiency of general waste management. At that time, Bangladesh had no regulation-based incentives for end-of-pipe (EOP) waste treatment, so we expected the enterprises to have invested little in such efforts. We were wrong.

Despite their operational similarities, the factories' EOP treatment and pollution varied widely.

NGFF (Natural Gas Fertilizer Factory, Sylhet) was Bangladesh's oldest urea fertilizer plant, built with Japanese assistance in 1961. Downstream villages had clearly identified the plant's discharges as the cause of fish kills, paddy-field damage, and health threats. Yet community pressure for change was only moderate, as the area is primarily nonindustrial and offers few other factory jobs. BCIC, too, regarded the facility as obsolete and kept it open only to preserve the local employment base. Everyone recognized that the age and technology of the plant precluded cleanup to a high standard, so nearby communities settled for some compensation and a first-level cleanup effort.

Figure B1.1   Plants in Bangladesh

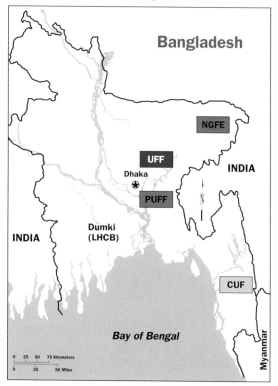

UFF and **PUFF** (Urea and Potash Urea Fertilizer Factories, Narsingdi) were built in different eras: UFF with Japanese assistance in 1968, and PUFF with Chinese assistance in 1985. Technologically, however, they were roughly at parity because the Chinese design closely reflected the two-decades-old Japanese design. Both plants were clearly identifiable polluters whose damage intensity fell in the mid range of our survey. Downstream fish kills and paddy damage from polluted irrigation water were common, and the community exerted strong

Box 1.1 *(continued)*

pressure for cleanup in the 1980s, emboldened by the relative abundance of other local jobs. In response, UFF increased the number of employees working on pollution control, and both plants paid some compensation for damage claims. The two plants also shared a first-stage treatment lagoon, constructed by UFF in 1980. Both factories used the lagoon to dilute the effluent with wastewater from their employee housing complexes. UFF also used urea hydrolysis, an ion exchange facility, and an oil/grease separation plant to clean up its effluent. PUFF, in turn, reduced the ammonia load in its effluent with a steam stripping method, and spread a simple cloth barrier over the outfall to capture some of the oil and grease.

CUF (Chittagong Urea Factory, Chittagong) was the country's newest, largest, and most advanced urea fertilizer factory. Because it was constructed in 1989 with Japanese assistance and incorporated modern Japanese technology, CUF was a very clean plant. A treatment lagoon had been excavated, but the effluent load was so low that the plant discharged wastewater directly into the Karnaphuli River. Although local employment alternatives were plentiful, neighboring communities had put no pressure on CUF, as they considered its environmental controls acceptable. These controls surpassed any regulatory standards that the Government of Bangladesh was likely to enforce in the coming decade.

These findings suggest that an intriguing and hopeful story is unfolding in the developing world. Long before reaching middle-income status, countries like Indonesia, Philippines, and Bangladesh have begun an environmental transition in which some factories are demonstrating high levels of environmental performance.

The role of economic development in this transition is clearly revealed by a study based on reports submitted to the 1992 U.N. Conference on Environment and Development held in Rio de Janeiro (Dasgupta, Mody, Roy, and Wheeler, 1995). The research shows a continuous relationship between national income per capita and the strictness of environmental regulation (Figure 1.4, Box 1.2). According to a recent World Bank study, the result is a 1 percent decline in the intensity of organic water pollution—the amount per unit of industrial output—for each 1 percent increase in income per capita. The study is based on extensive data from environmental agencies in Brazil, China, Finland, India, Indonesia, Korea, Mexico, the Netherlands, Philippines, Sri Lanka, Taiwan (China), Thailand, and the United States.[2] Overall, the data reveal that pollution intensity falls by 90 percent as per capita income rises from $500 to $20,000 (Figure 1.5). Most important, the fastest decline occurs *before* countries reach middle-income status.

Figure 1.4   Regulation vs. Income

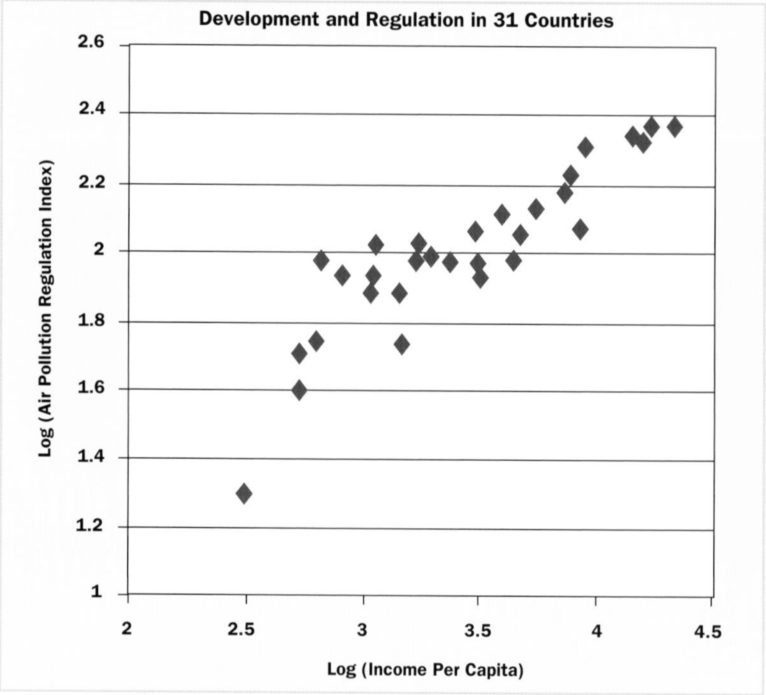

Source: Dasgupta, Mody, Roy, and Wheeler (1995)

Table 1.1   Sectoral Indices of Organic Water Pollution Intensity

Sector	Index
Food	100
Pulp and Paper	87
Chemicals	29
Textiles	26
Wood Products	13
Metal Products	8
Metals	3
Nonmetallic Minerals	2

Source: Hettige, Mani, and Wheeler (1998)

However, total pollution in developing countries could still rise if industrial output grows faster than pollution intensity declines. This is especially true because development affects the share of an economy's polluting industries. An economy that depends largely on food and paper production, for example, poses a much greater threat of organic water pollution than one based on metals and nonmetallic minerals (Table 1.1). Yet an analysis of data from more than one hundred countries reveals that development shifts production to sectors that produce *less* organic water pollution per unit of output. This shift toward cleaner sectors reduces overall water pollution intensity by 30 percent as income rises to around $5,000 per capita (Figure 1.6).

We still need to estimate total organic water pollution in each sector of growing economies, to determine whether industrial expansion yields more waste. Such estimates are difficult to find, so to produce them we have used another result from the 12-country study cited above. In those countries, we found that for each 1 percent rise in per capita income (and wages), labor intensity also

Box 1.2 Environmental Regulation and Economic Development

We have analyzed international differences in environmental regulation using reports presented to the United Nations Conference on Environment and Development (UNCED, 1992) by 145 countries. The UNCED reports are similar in form as well as coverage, and permit cross-country comparisons. To an impressive degree, they seem to reflect real environmental conditions and issues.

From the information in these reports, we have developed a set of indicators that measure the status of pollution control policy and performance in 31 randomly selected coun-

tries. Our survey assessment uses a variety of questions to categorize the (i) scope of policies adopted; (ii) scope of legislation enacted; (iii) control mechanisms in place; and (iv) degree of success in implementation. The status in each category is graded "high, medium, or low," with assigned values of 2, 1, and 0 respectively. We have developed over 500 assessment scores for each country and computed separate composite indices of regulations for air and water pollution. The resulting index values increase continuously with national income per capita.

Income and Environmental Regulation

Country	GNP Per Capita ($1990)	Air Regulation Index	Water Regulation Index	Country	GNP Per Capita ($1990)	Air Regulation Index	Water Regulation Index
Mozambique	80	56	98	Paraguay	1,110	84	117
Tanzania	110	50	90	Jordan	1,240	95	131
Ethiopia	120	20	56	Thailand	1,420	98	113
Bhutan	190	39	54	Tunisia	1,440	128	158
Malawi	200	93	116	Jamaica	1,500	114	168
Bangladesh	210	77	89	Bulgaria	2,250	168	198
Nigeria	290	75	106	South Africa	2,530	136	165
India	350	105	132	Brazil	2,680	113	127
China	370	98	127	Trinidad	3,610	118	149
Kenya	370	85	127	Korea	5,400	150	170
Pakistan	380	105	131	Ireland	9,550	203	223
Ghana	390	93	124	Netherlands	17,320	219	226
Zambia	420	87	115	Germany	22,320	236	242
Egypt	600	92	134	Finland	26,040	214	229
Philippines	730	93	113	Switzerland	32,680	231	240
Papua New Guinea	860	54	91				

Source: Dasgupta, Mody, Roy, and Wheeler (1995)

Figure 1.5   Per Capita Income and Industrial Pollution

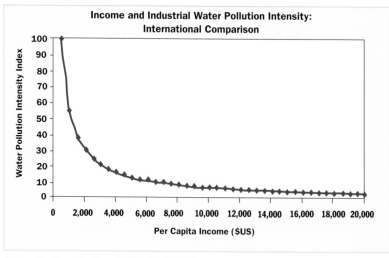

Source: Hettige, Mani, and Wheeler (1998)

Figure 1.6   Economic Development and Sectoral Change

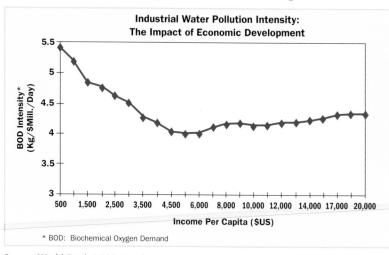

Source: World Bank BESD Database; Hettige, Mani, and Wheeler (1998)

declines by approximately 1 percent. As countries grow richer, rising wages lead to lower demand for labor per unit of output.

The study shows that economic development has a parallel impact on organic water pollution intensity: Stricter regulation and greater productive efficiency lead to lower pollution per unit of output. As a result, an average Indian paper mill employs far more workers and generates far more pollution than a U.S. mill with the same capacity. But because labor and water pollution intensities decline at about the same rate with development, the two mills have similar pollution/labor ratios.

We can use these results to estimate total industrial water pollution loads for a variety of countries, using a U.N. database that provides annual employment figures for each industry sector and country. For example, to estimate organic water pollution from paper production in each country, we multiply that country's paper-sector employment by our estimated (constant) pollution/labor ratio for the paper sector. We multiply employment in the metals sector by its pollution/labor ratio, and similarly for all other industry sectors. Then we add across sectors to obtain total estimated organic water pollution for each country.

To determine the relationship between economic development and total organic water pollution during the 1970s and 1980s, we have selected 15 countries within four major economic groups: the Organisation for Economic Co-operation and Development (or OECD), represented by the United States, Japan, France, and Germany; the newly industrialized economies (or NIEs), represented by Mexico, Brazil, Taiwan (China), Korea, South Africa, and Turkey; the less-developed countries of Asia (or LDCs), represented by China, India, and Indonesia; and the ex-COMECON countries, represented by Poland and the former Soviet Union.

In the OECD countries, despite continued economic growth, we estimate that total organic water pollution declined by 4 percent from 1977 to 1989 (Table 1.2), reflecting rising per capita income and more regulation. Organic water pollution in the NIEs increased by about 40 percent, while in the poorer Asian countries it grew at a slightly higher rate—49 percent. Since the latter three countries are very large, we estimate that they generated most of the pollution growth in our international sample (Table 1.2). The OECD and ex-COMECON countries dropped significantly in their share of pollution, while the NIEs increased their share only marginally.

Perhaps most impressive is our estimate that total organic water pollution from industry grew by only 16 percent in these 15 major industrial countries. Although economic growth sparked fears of skyrocketing pollution in the 1970s and 1980s, development was setting the stage for real improvements in environmental performance.

Table 1.2   Trends in Organic Water Pollution: Selected Countries, 1977–1989

Region	Emissions ('000 Kg/Day)					% Ch. 1977–89
	1977	1980	1983	1986	1989	
OECD	5,776	5,847	5,501	5,403	5,523	–4
COMECON	4,127	4,218	4,302	4,228	4,039	–2
NIEs	1,565	1,917	1,848	2,197	2,188	40
ASIAN LDCs	4,617	5,030	5,566	6,183	6,883	49
TOTAL	16,085	17,012	17,217	18,011	18,633	16
	% of Total Pollution					
	1977	1980	1983	1986	1989	
OECD	36	34	32	30	30	
COMECON	26	25	25	23	22	
NIEs	10	11	11	12	12	
ASIAN LDCs	29	30	32	34	37	

Source: Hettige, Mani, and Wheeler (1998)

1.4 The Rise and Fall of Pollution Havens

The pattern of international trade provides another measure of this record. Northern environmental groups have long expressed the concern that poor countries will become pollution havens, attracting industries that relocate from richer countries to avoid strict regulations, and siphoning away jobs in the process. Yet a look at overall trade statistics shows that permanent pollution havens have not emerged.

Concern about pollution havens began in the early 1970s, when developed countries rapidly tightened pollution controls and most developing countries had not yet begun formal regulation. Business investment in pollution controls skyrocketed in Japan during that time (Figure 1.7), and companies in North America and Western Europe made similar investments. If such costs gave an edge to polluting industries in developing countries, the effect should have appeared in international trade patterns: Developing countries' exports of the products of dirty industries should have risen faster than their imports, lowering their import/export ratios for these products. The converse should have been true for developed countries.

Figure 1.7   Pollution Control Investment in Japan

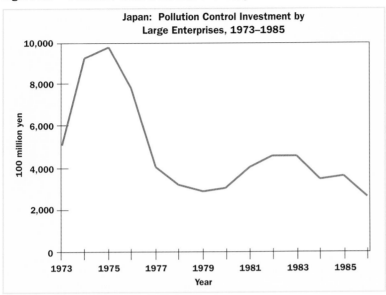

Source: Mani and Wheeler (1998)

Figure 1.8 shows that the shadow of pollution havens did emerge in five particularly polluting sectors: iron and steel, nonferrous metals, industrial chemicals, pulp and paper, and nonmetallic mineral products.[3] After the early 1970s, Japan's import/export ratio in these industries rose rapidly, while the ratio declined steeply in the newly industrialized economies (NIEs) of the Republic of Korea, Taiwan (China), Singapore, and Hong Kong (China). And the same pattern occurred in mainland China and the other developing countries of East Asia a decade later. However, in each region the pollution haven story was markedly short. Both sets of Asian economies have stabilized their import/export ratios at levels greater than one, and remain net importers of pollution-intensive products from industrial countries.

The story in the Western Hemisphere is similar. In North America, the United States and Canada witnessed a steady climb in import/export ratios for polluting industries from the beginning of the environmental era to the late 1980s, while Latin America experienced the opposite after 1973. However, as in developing Asia, the Latin American ratio leveled off near one by the 1990s.

Why didn't polluting industries continue to shift to developing countries? Economic growth—accompanied by more regulation—provides the best answer. Along with greater prosperity in the newly

Figure 1.8   Import/Export Ratio Trends for Polluting Industries

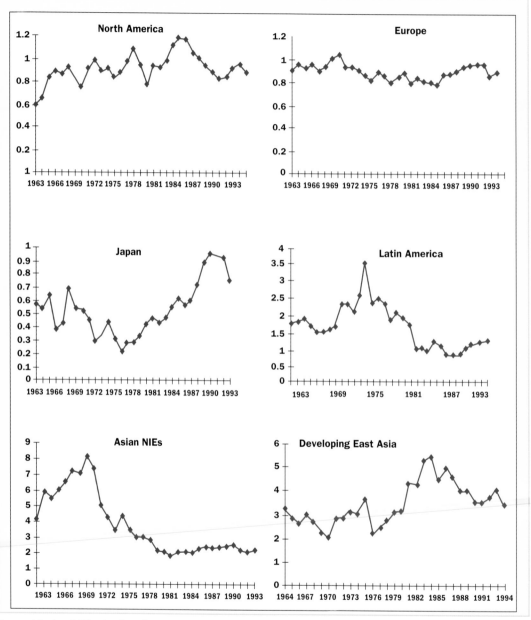

Source: Mani and Wheeler (1998)

industrialized countries came increased demands for environmental quality and better institutional capacity to regulate. The same process occurred in the Asian developing countries after a decade's delay. Faced with rising costs from environmental damage, they stabilized the terms of trade through measures to control their own pollution.

1.5 Controlling Pollution: Benefits and Costs

Poor countries are taking more steps to control pollution, but they must carefully justify such efforts because resources used to curb emissions could also be used to build schools or train doctors. Yet environmental policymakers in developing countries who look closely at the benefits and costs of controlling pollution are moving toward even stronger support for regulation.

China provides an excellent case in point. Output from the country's 10 million industrial enterprises grew by more than 15 percent annually during the 1990s, and industry is China's largest productive sector, accounting for 47 percent of its gross domestic product and employing 17 percent of the country's labor force. Despite the country's progress in controlling pollution, serious environmental damage has undeniably accompanied this rapid growth. As we have noted, China's State Environmental Protection Agency (SEPA) estimates that industry accounts for over 70 percent of the nation's organic water pollution, sulfur dioxide (SO_2) emissions, and flue dust. Atmospheric concentrations of suspended particulates and SO_2 in urban areas routinely exceed World Health Organization safety standards by large margins.

China's pollution problem is clearly compelling, but how much more pollution control can the Chinese afford to undertake? To begin to weigh benefits and costs, a team of Chinese researchers has estimated the link between air pollution and mortality from respiratory disease in Beijing.[4] Their analysis shows that a "statistical life" could be saved by removing 100 tons of SO_2 annually from Beijing's atmosphere (Box 1.3).

But how much would it cost to abate those 100 tons of SO_2? To find out, we estimated abatement costs for large and small plants in China: Figure 1.9 shows the incremental cost per ton of pollutant removed as the degree of abatement rises. The scales on the vertical axes of the two graphs indicate that small plants have much higher marginal abatement costs than large plants, and that state-owned

Box 1.3 Controlling Air Pollution and Saving Lives in Beijing

Xu et al. (1994) have estimated dose-response relationships linking atmospheric pollution to respiratory disease in Beijing. Their study shows that atmospheric sulfur dioxide (SO_2) concentration is highly correlated with damage from respiratory disease. Recent scientific evidence provides some insight into the nature of this relationship. Sulfur dioxide and other oxides of sulfur combine with oxygen to form sulfates, and with water vapor to form aerosols of sulfurous and sulfuric acid. These acid mists can irritate the respiratory systems of humans and animals. Therefore, a high concentration of SO_2 can affect breathing, and may aggravate existing respiratory and cardiovascular diseases. Sensitive populations include asthmatics, individuals with bronchitis or emphysema, children, and the elderly.

The second, and probably more significant, effect of SO_2 is traceable to the impact of fine particulates on mortality and morbidity. A review of recent evidence by the U.S. Environmental Protection Agency suggests that fine particulates are the source of the worst health damage from air pollution. In the case of China, there is reason to believe that 30 to 40 percent of fine particulates are in the form of sulfates from SO_2 emissions.

In 1993, Beijing had a population of about 11,120,000; the mortality rate was about 0.611 percent; total deaths were about 68,000; and total SO_2 emissions were about 366 thousand tons (of which 204 thousand were from industry). From this base, a decrease of 1,000 tons in SO_2 emissions decreases total emissions by $1/366 \times 100$ percent. An independent econometric analysis of the relationship between emissions and air pollution in China's cities predicts an associated decrease of $0.51 \times 1/366 \times 100$ percent in Beijing's ambient SO_2 concentration. Applying the Beijing dose-response result of Xu et al. to the new concentration, we obtain an estimated saving of 10.4 lives per year. Dividing both elements by 10 yields a useful round number for policy discussion: 1 life saved per 100 tons abated annually.

Source: Dasgupta, Wang, and Wheeler (1997)

enterprises (SOEs) have far higher marginal abatement costs than other plants.

As large plants are a major source of air pollution in cities like Beijing, the numbers for those facilities are particularly interesting. Our results show that abating one ton of SO_2, when 10 percent of emissions are controlled, would cost large plants about US$3. This is very low by international standards: U.S. environmental policymakers have been happy to discover that industry can abate SO_2 for less than $100 per ton. If abating 100 tons—at a cost of $300—will save a life, can anyone seriously argue that it shouldn't be done? In China, the numbers are clearly signaling that pollution control is far too lax.

To consider how much further pollution control should be tightened, a simple exercise in valuation is worthwhile. In the West, environmental agencies commonly use a value of at least $1,000,000 to

Figure 1.9   The Cost of Air Pollution Control in China

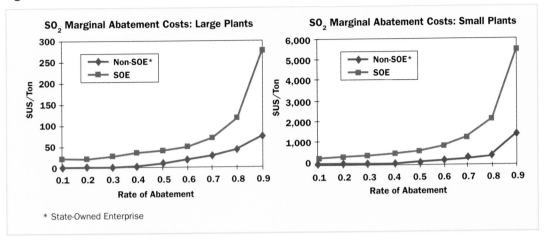

Source: Dasgupta, Wang, and Wheeler (1997)

assess the social benefit when pollution control saves one life. In Beijing, it costs only $300 to save a life by abating 100 tons of SO_2. Using the Western benefit standard, the implied benefit-cost ratio (1,000,000/300) is over 3,000 : 1. Some analysts have proposed much lower benefit estimates for China, but a figure as low as $8,000 would still yield a benefit-cost ratio of 24 : 1. In either case, the implied social rate of return for air pollution abatement is extremely high. China's regulators have reduced air pollution significantly by charging factories for their emissions (see Chapter 2). Yet even for a life-benefit value of only $8,000, we estimate that returns to further abatement are high enough to justify a 50-fold increase in the pollution charge rate.

Of course, environmental, social, and economic conditions will yield different conclusions in different countries and regions. But efforts to apply the same methods to countries as varied as Brazil and Indonesia have yielded similar results: When the benefits of reduced pollution are weighed against the costs of control, today's regulation appears far too lax.[5] Pollution control is a very attractive option for saving lives in the large cities of developing countries.

1.6 The New Agenda

The record shows that developing countries are not destined to be the world's environmental dumping grounds: Even the most polluted areas are moving away from the nightmare landscapes anticipated only a few years ago. In China, air pollution has been stable or dropping during the past decade despite a rapid increase in income, and we see strong evidence that economic development boosts pollution control elsewhere in the developing world. Regulation has grown steadily with income, and its impact has quickly reduced the pollution intensity of industrial production.

Yet benefit-cost studies in Asia and Latin America show that pollution damage remains unjustifiably heavy, given the low cost of abatement. More action is needed on three fronts: regulatory reform, economic policy reform, and better environmental management within factories. On the regulatory front, new, surprisingly low-cost strategies based on pollution charges and public information have reduced emissions from many factories. We take a detailed look at these strategies in Chapters 2, 3, and 4, drawing on new research and examples of imaginative and effective programs in developing countries. In addition, we explore the complex real-world decision making that these programs try to reflect. Chapter 4 also looks inside the factory gate for more clues to effective pollution fighting. Recent policy experiments suggest that pollution falls significantly when environmental agencies broaden their mandate to include technical assistance to plant managers in the private sector. Chapter 5 explores the effects of economic reforms, such as privatization, market liberalization, and curtailment of subsidies for materials and fuels, to determine which can best be used to prevent pollution.

Regulatory and economic policy reforms do not take place in a vacuum: in Chapter 6, we identify political and institutional changes needed to support such efforts. In-depth research on these changes is lacking, because most relevant knowledge is in the heads of the people who are leading the process of policy innovation in developing countries. We have been fortunate enough to work with many of them, and this chapter presents the lessons they have taught us.

Finally, in Chapter 7, we summarize the main findings of this report and highlight the keys to progress. We see an urgent need for expanding the pilot projects we describe and disseminating their lessons internationally, and we hope this report will contribute to such efforts. We also suggest useful roles for our own institution in promoting the new agenda. On balance, given the recent record, we remain optimistic about the prospect for continued progress in controlling industrial pollution.

References

Calkins, R., et al., 1994, "Indonesia: Environment and Development" (Washington: World Bank).

Dasgupta, S., A. Mody, S. Roy, and D. Wheeler, 1995, "Environmental Regulation and Development: A Cross-Country Empirical Analysis," World Bank Policy Research Department Working Paper, No. 1448, March.

Dasgupta, S., H. Wang, and D. Wheeler, 1997, "Surviving Success: Policy Reform and the Future of Industrial Pollution in China," World Bank Policy Research Department Working Paper, No. 1856, October.

Hartman, R., M. Singh, and D. Wheeler, 1997, "The Cost of Air Pollution Abatement," *Applied Economics,* Vol. 29, No. 6.

Hettige, H., M. Mani, and D. Wheeler, 1998, "Industrial Pollution in Economic Development: Kuznets Revisited," World Bank Development Research Group Working Paper, No. 1876, January.

Huq, M., and D. Wheeler, 1992, "Pollution Reduction Without Formal Regulation: Evidence from Bangladesh," World Bank Environment Department Working Paper, No. 1992-39.

Mani, M., and D. Wheeler, 1998, "In Search of Pollution Havens? Dirty Industry in the World Economy, 1960–1995," *Journal of Environment and Development,* Vol. 7, No. 3.

Von Amsberg, J., 1997, "Brazil: Managing Pollution Problems, The Brown Environmental Agenda," World Bank Report No. 16635-BR, June.

Xu, X., J. Gao, D. Dockery, and Y. Chen, 1994, "Air Pollution and Daily Mortality in Residential Areas of Beijing, China," *Archives of Environmental Health,* Vol. 49, No. 4, 216–22.

End Notes

1. Indonesia and Philippines have nearly identical color coding schemes, permitting direct comparison of results in Figure 1.3.

2. See Hettige, Mani, and Wheeler (1998).

3. See Mani and Wheeler (1998).

4. See Xu et al. (1994).

5. Similar case studies for Brazil and Indonesia, respectively, are available in Von Amsberg (1997) and Calkins (1994).

Colombia's Rio Negro

Source: *David Shaman*

Chapter Two

Regulating Pollution in the Real World

R ising in the Andean highlands, the rivers of Colombia's Antioquia region tumble wild and clean as they begin their descent to the Caribbean. The headwaters pass through upland ecosystems whose variety makes Colombia a world treasure of biodiversity. As the highlands give way to broad valleys, the rivers of Antioquia flow more slowly past human settlements. Their sparkle fades as wastes pour in from farms, factories, and towns along their banks. Before the waters reach the sea, their life-sustaining oxygen is depleted and their beds are laced with toxic metals. Sustainers of richly varied life in the highlands, they become purveyors of death in their encounters with human society in the lowlands.

Economic development has not been kind to Colombia's rivers. Regulations have stipulated limits on discharges for decades, and Colombians have supported corrective action, but polluters have flouted these regulations for just as long. Yet in the early 1990s community support for cleaner rivers finally crystallized into demands for reform. The result is one of the world's most innovative programs for controlling pollution. Its governing maxim is simple: All polluters—towns, factories, and farms—must pay for each unit of organic pollution they discharge into the waterways of the Antioquia district.

The result? Reported organic discharges have dropped by 18 percent during the program's first year. The most striking change has occurred along the Rio Negro, where factories have accounted for over 40 percent of organic pollution: These factories have reduced their organic discharges by 52 percent.

Colombia's recent experience reflects a movement toward regulatory reform throughout the developing world. Decades of attempts to control pollution through traditional regulations, which make discharges above designated limits illegal, have often yielded disappointing results. Under traditional regulation, pollution above the legal limit is punishable by fines, plant shutdowns, or, in extreme cases, imprisonment of offending managers. But such an approach requires strong enforcement mechanisms: Regulators have to monitor and analyze pollution from each plant, determine whether it has violated the rules, and institute legal proceedings in cases where violation is clear. These steps are not cheap, and many developing countries have not been able to implement them. What's more, such a system requires every commercial enterprise to toe the same regulatory line regardless of cost.

In an effort to break out of this one-size-fits-all approach, many countries are opting for more flexible and efficient regulation that nevertheless provides strong incentives for polluters to change their ways. Some countries have chosen strategies for traditional regulation that take benefits and costs into account. Some are using pollution charges like those in Colombia—often combined with other strategies—to achieve impressive results. Still others, discussed in Chapter 3, are using public disclosure programs that pressure polluters to clean up their act.

2.1 The Role of Economic Incentives

We begin with an obvious but important proposition: Plant managers respond mainly to economic incentives. Although public spirit moves a notable minority to control pollution, most managers are bound by pressures from markets and shareholders. They will reduce discharges only if they expect the additional cost to be less than the penalties that continued pollution will impose on them. Such penalties can include not only fines and plant closures but also pollution charges, credit refusals from bankers worried about liability, reduced sales to consumers who care about the environment, and even social ostracism within communities outraged about pollution.

However, a manager's situation is uncertain because a plant's emissions vary daily, local regulators may be spread too thin to enforce penalties, and reactions from markets and communities are unpredictable. Managers must find the right balance between the possibility of heavy penalties from too much pollution and the certainty of high costs from too much abatement. Understanding this balancing act is the key to more effective regulation.

Figure 2.1 shows why this is not a simple problem. The figure portrays information on the concentration of organic pollution in emissions from a large Indonesian factory during 1994 and 1995. At the beginning of a public disclosure program in June 1995, Indonesian regulators privately notified the plant's managers that they had received a poor rating because their average daily pollution exceeded Indonesia's legal standard of 300 milligrams per liter for that industry sector. Faced with the threat of public disclosure, the managers quickly installed equipment designed to reduce concentration to around 100 milligrams per liter. By late November, the plant had

Figure 2.1   Normal Variations in Emissions

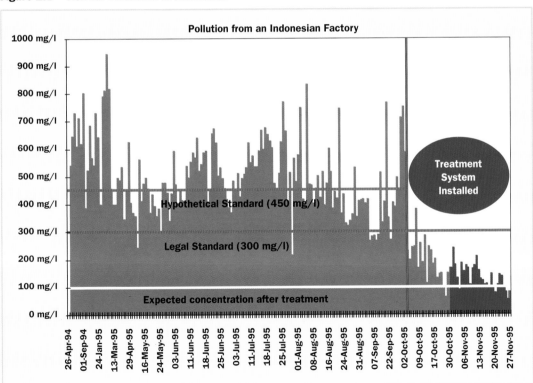

Source: BAPEDAL

29

moved down the learning curve sufficiently to bring its typical emissions into the 100 milligrams per liter range.

Yet Figure 2.1 shows that even before the treatment equipment was installed, effluent concentrations occasionally dipped below the legal standard. Suppose the standard had been 450 milligrams per liter—would the plant have been in compliance? The answer would have been no if regulators had insisted that all daily observations fall below the standard. Yet if regulators had averaged emissions over time, they might have judged the plant compliant.

Faced with such variation, regulators and plant managers alike find themselves in a complex game.[1] Inspectors need enough information to establish a characteristic pollution level. They would like the cooperation of plant management, since managers can easily delay or complicate the regulatory process. For their part, managers have no interest in antagonizing inspectors; because once a plant has become suspect, regulators will demand time-consuming and costly investigations and reports. However, managers will also tend to rationalize strings of bad observations as anomalies, and in some cases they will undoubtedly be justified. The result is that uncertainty reigns, and regulation involves continual negotiation.

The Regulator's Dilemma

Figure 2.2 illustrates the fundamental dilemma regulators must confront—as well as a way of resolving it. The red line shows that each additional (or marginal) unit of pollution creates more damage than the previous unit—progressively more respiratory disease from air pollution, fewer fish in contaminated water, etc. This is called the marginal social damage (MSD) schedule.

Pollution abatement is subject to the opposite effect—a law of diminishing returns. As the blue line shows, each additional (or marginal) unit of pollution control costs more than the previous unit. This graph is the marginal abatement cost (MAC) schedule. It shows that pollution control can be cheap at low levels of abatement but expensive at high levels.

If regulators target the brown level of pollution, the marginal cost of abatement will be much lower than the marginal social damage. This means that reductions in damage through pollution control will more than compensate for increases in abatement costs. The opposite will be true for the yellow level of pollution, where MAC is much higher than MSD. The optimal choice for regulators is the green level of pollution, where MAC and MSD are equal. At this

Figure 2.2   Abatement Benefits and Costs

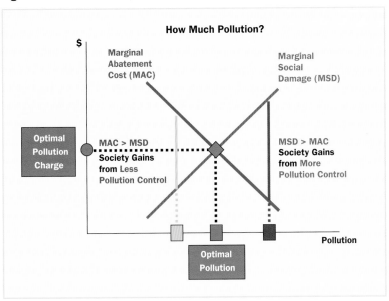

point, neither increasing nor decreasing pollution will improve overall social welfare.

MAC vs. MEP: The Manager's Dilemma

Figure 2.3 illustrates the complex decisions factory managers face in weighing the penalties for polluting. The factory's cost is measured on the vertical axis, and pollution per unit of output (or pollution intensity) on the horizontal axis.[2] The two upward-sloping lines show that marginal expected pollution penalties (MEP) increase as pollution intensity rises. That's because even weak regulators are bound to take notice if the plant's pollution intensity exceeds the legal limit by a wide margin. And even if regulators do not enforce legal standards, communities and markets will exact penalties from obvious, heavy polluters. The green and red MEP lines reflect differences in the strength of local regulation and the quality of information on the factory's pollution available to banks, consumers, and local communities.

Confronted with green or red MEP, a cost-minimizing manager needs information about abatement costs before deciding how much to pollute. Figure 2.4 illustrates the cost problem for two different

Figure 2.3   Penalties for Polluting

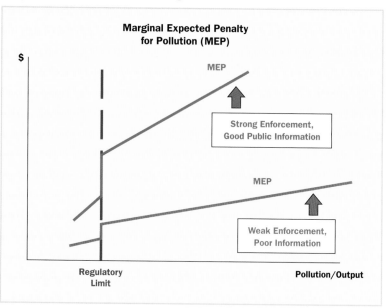

Figure 2.4   Abatement Cost

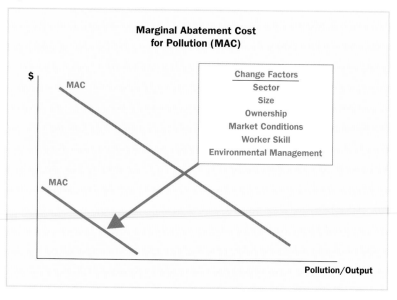

factories. The red factory incurs much more cost than the green factory, although each incremental unit of abatement costs more for
both. Recent research, discussed in later chapters, suggests that the
lower MAC of the green plant correlates with factors such as larger

size, ownership by a private, multi-plant company, better-educated workers, and better environmental management.

Figure 2.5 combines the red MAC with the green MEP to show how a manager can choose to react to penalties and abatement costs. At the brown level of pollution intensity, MEP is much higher than MAC, so the manager can lower costs by reducing pollution. At the green level of pollution intensity, MAC is much higher than MEP, so the manager can lower costs by reducing pollution control activity. The manager's cost-minimizing choice is the yellow level of pollution intensity, where MAC and MEP are equal. At this level, neither increasing nor decreasing pollution will lower a plant's overall costs.

Why Compliance Varies So Widely

Our model of cost-minimizing pollution shows why plants in developing countries vary widely in complying with regulation, even where it is weak. In Figure 2.6, the pairs of MAC and MEP schedules intersect at four points, colored green, blue, yellow, and red. The red (or "outlaw") case occurs when a plant with high MAC faces a weak

Figure 2.5   Plant-Level Pollution

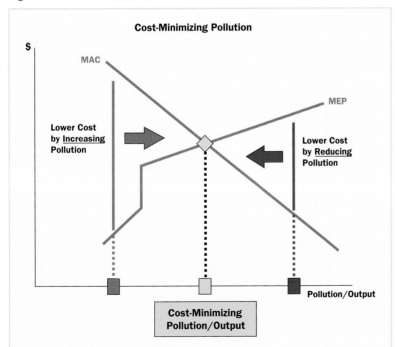

Figure 2.6   Cost-Minimizing Pollution Choices

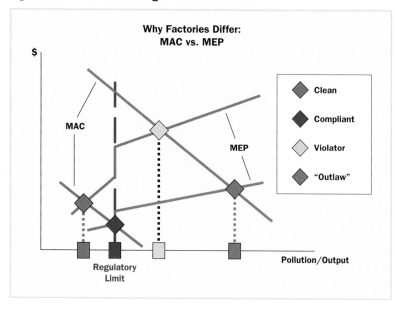

regulatory and information environment in which MEP is low. Such a plant will pollute heavily.

Strengthening regulation and public information will shift the MEP schedule from red to green and motivate the plant manager to lower overall costs by reducing pollution intensity to the yellow level. At this level, the plant still exceeds the legally permissible (blue) limit but by much less than in the red case.

In contrast, even weak regulation can induce compliance if changes in a plant lower its MAC. In Figure 2.6, the legal (blue) pollution limit occurs at the point where green MAC equals red MEP.

Recent research shows that plant managers sometimes reduce pollution below the blue point required by law, given other pressures from communities and markets (Chapter 3). In Figure 2.6, this occurs where green MEP equals green MAC.

Chapter 1 has shown that more pollution control can yield a large social payoff in many developing-country cities. This entails shifting the industry mix from plants that are predominantly red and yellow to those that are predominantly blue and green. As Figure 2.6 shows, this can be achieved by changing MEP, MAC, or both from red to green status. Policies that promote these changes work because they rely on plant managers' natural incentive to minimize their pollution-related costs.

2.2 Pollution Charges: The Right Solution?

Pollution charges, such as those imposed by Colombia, level the economic playing field by confronting all managers with the same price for each unit of pollution. Under such a system, managers are free to adjust their operations until they have minimized pollution-related costs—charges plus the cost of abatement. This system minimizes overall abatement costs while providing the right incentives for managers to clean up. Yet at first glance a charge system looks unnecessarily complicated. Why not just require all factories to cut back pollution by the same uniform percentage until overall pollution falls to the desired level? That system can also work, but it will heavily penalize factories with high marginal abatement costs.

The challenge is to set pollution charges that promote the right level of cleanup from society's perspective. A recent study for Zhengzhou, the capital of Henan province in central China, shows how regulators can do so if they have good information. With a 1993 population of 1.8 million and an average industrial wage of 3,350 yuan per year, Zhengzhou is typical of China's large cities. Its industry pours approximately 45,000 tons of sulfur dioxide (SO_2) into the atmosphere every year, contributing to an ambient SO_2 concentration of 90 micrograms per cubic meter. At this level, over 400 Zhengzhou residents die annually from SO_2-related pollution, and thousands suffer from serious respiratory illness.

At current emissions (100 on the horizontal axis), Figure 2.7 suggests that the benefit from abating an additional ton of SO_2—that is, reducing the marginal social damage—is $50, while the cost of abating it is $1.70. This illustrative case uses $8,000 as an extremely conservative estimate of the social benefit from saving a life through air pollution control. Figures in excess of $1,000,000 could be employed, as we note in Chapter 1. However, even a rock-bottom value of $8,000 implies that about 70 percent of today's emissions should be eliminated to achieve the social optimum.

The charge that will induce this reduction is about $90 per ton, at the intersection of MAC and MSD.[3] This is the optimum charge for Zhengzhou, since a lower charge would leave socially profitable abatement opportunities unexploited, and a higher charge would impose an abatement cost higher than the social gain from further cuts in pollution.

This analysis suggests that the air pollution charge should be increased more than fiftyfold in Zhengzhou and, by implication, the rest

Figure 2.7   Optimal Pollution

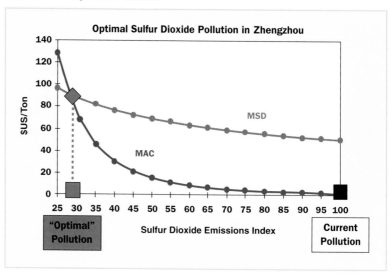

of urban China. As we saw in Chapter 1, the current pollution charge makes sense only if China's policymakers value the life of an average urban resident at less than $300. For the loss of a human life, this figure seems ludicrously low compared with the pain, suffering, and elimination of a lifetime's contribution to China's economic output.

A pollution charge not only cuts emissions but generates public revenue as well. If Zhengzhou's environmental regulators increased the SO_2 levy to $90 per ton, the city's annual revenue from air pollution charges would be approximately $1.1 million. For China as a whole, revenue from an SO_2 charge of $90 per ton would be about $250 million—even then, only a small fraction of the charge's value as a lifesaving policy tool.

Pollution Charges in Practice

Why does pollution control in China and elsewhere fall short of the social optimum, as in the Zhengzhou case? Good studies of emissions and the damage they cause are still limited to a few air pollutants—principally particulates and sulfur dioxide—in a few cities. Guesstimates must be employed for water pollution and hazardous waste.

As with traditional regulations, effective monitoring, and enforcement of pollution charges can also be costly and time consuming. Claims from industry representatives about the excessive cost of regulation may be well received by high-level policymakers who are not informed about the benefits of controlling pollution. And arguments against charging for illegal pollution are also common on the grounds that criminal acts should be punished, not merely subjected to fees.

Thus, although the "golden rule" MAC = MSD provides a good framework for determining environmental goals and pollution charges, in the real world the actual levels are determined through the political process. Concrete information about lives lost, fisheries destroyed, and other damage can play some role, but it will never be the sole determining factor. Policymakers have to seek consensus on environmental goals and then use the available regulatory instruments to pursue them.

In the 1970s, economists William Baumol and Wallace Oates wrote a classic book showing how pollution charges could be adapted to these political realities.[4] They recommended a four-step approach: 1. Determine environmental quality goals; 2. Estimate the pollution reduction required by these goals; 3. Estimate the marginal cost of abatement at the desired level of pollution; 4. Set the pollution charge equal to the estimated marginal cost. If the estimate is right, pollution should fall to the desired level. If it is wrong, the charge can be raised if there is too little abatement and reduced if there is too much.

Baumol and Oates have joined other public-finance economists in arguing that all revenues from such a system should be rebated to the central treasury, where they can be allocated to the highest-priority spending categories. These categories might be environmental, but they might also include health care, education, transportation, and other public-sector responsibilities.

Has any developing country—or, for that matter, any industrial country—actually instituted an ideal charge system? The answer is no, but some countries have come close. Box 2.1 describes a long-established pollution charge system in the Netherlands, which has applied this economic instrument more successfully than most other OECD countries. Several developing countries have also used charges to regulate pollution. Their experiences illustrate the problems and potential of this economic instrument as a regulatory tool for newly industrializing countries.

(1) Colombia

Colombia experienced a lamentable lack of success with traditional regulation, and contamination of its air and water long went practically unchecked. In a strong attempt to break with the past,

Box 2.1 Dutch Pollution Charges: An "Accidental" Success Story

Among the OECD countries, the Netherlands has had the most extensive and successful experience with charges for water pollution.[5] By 1969, organic water pollution had mounted to the point where many Dutch waterways were biologically dead. Together industry and households were dumping 40 million population-equivalents, or PE—the average organic pollution caused by one person in a normal household—into Dutch sewers and waterways every year. Heavy-metals emissions from industry had also increased to dangerous levels.

The Dutch responded with the Pollution of Surface Waters Act (PSWA) in 1970, which prohibited unlicensed discharges into surface waters and imposed charges on polluting emissions. Industry had to pay for emissions of heavy metals, and all sectors of society were assessed for estimated organic discharges: urban households, 3 PE; farm households, 6 PE; small enterprises, 3 PE; medium enterprises, PE estimated from engineering models; and large enterprises, directly measured PE. Authorities granted rebates to small and medium enterprises if they could prove that their actual emissions were lower than official estimates.

The Dutch system began as a command-and-control exercise, in which pollution charges were simply intended to finance construction of waste treatment facilities mandated by the PSWA. However, pollution-reduction efforts required construction of high-cost facilities in some areas, and charges escalated as construction costs mounted. At some point, many Dutch factory managers found themselves confronted

Figure B2.1 The Impact of Dutch Pollution Charges

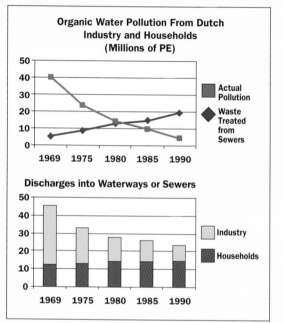

with charges equal to marginal abatement costs at very high levels of cleanup. A careful statistical analysis by Bressers (1988) has shown that these high charges were much more important than the permitting process in promoting reductions in emissions. By 1990, the system had halved both heavy-metals emissions and total organic discharges into waterways and sewers, and waste treatment facilities had expanded sufficiently to reduce organic pollution of waterways to about 6 million PE. Industry displayed the strongest response to pollution charges from 1969 to 1990, reducing its annual organic emissions from 33.0 to 8.8 million PE (Jansen, 1991).

the country based its new pollution charge system on the Baumol/Oates principles. Analysis of abatement costs concluded that a charge of US$100 per ton would reduce industry's organic emissions to Colombia's waterways by 80 percent. However, the program began by charging only US$28 per ton for organic waste (biochemical oxygen demand, or BOD), as well as $12 per ton for total suspended solids (TSS). These charges were considered high enough to bite, but not so costly as to provoke hostility from industry. The program will expand to include other pollutants based on the environmental and economic results of the first phase.

Seven regions in Colombia with the greatest population, economic activity and pollution are the flagships for implementing the charge system, and most other regions will begin participation during the next few years. Each region starts by setting its own pollution-reduction goals, imposing the national base charges, and tracking total discharges for six months. If the targets are not met, regional authorities can raise charges for the ensuing six months, and this process continues until local targets are met. At that point the charges are frozen, although adjusted to reflect inflation.

The pioneer in instituting this new program has been CORNARE, the pollution control authority in the Oriente Antioqueno region (Figure 2.8). CORNARE's dynamic leaders have forged a good working relationship with local businesses and communities. Before beginning the program, for example, the agency worked closely with several large factories to develop plans for installing cleaner technologies. CORNARE has also collected good information about local water pollution and thus can pinpoint the major sources of discharges into the Rio Negro and other rivers.

Industry is clearly the kingpin of water pollution in the region, followed by sewage from towns (Figure 2.9). After consulting with factory managers and communities, CORNARE set a reduction target of 50 percent for organic discharges. Although industry leaders protested that such an ambitious target would prove too costly, industry's recorded BOD discharges into the Rio Negro fell by 52 percent in the first six months under the plan, and TSS discharges fell by 16 percent. However, factories' responses varied widely: Of the 55 regulated plants on the Rio Negro, only 7 cut their recorded emissions of BOD, and only 8 cut TSS emissions. Obviously, the responsive plants reduced their pollution much more than average.

Table 2.1 shows that CORNARE's administration of pollution charges has been quite efficient: Assessed charges have been signifi-

Figure 2.8   CORNARE Region

cant, and collection rates have been high. Industries and municipalities have clearly gotten the message. So why have so few responded? One possibility is that the marginal cost of abatement remains above the charge for many factories, or managers may have simply not had enough time to adjust their pollution control practices. Indeed, CORNARE's director has noted that some plants that reduced pollu-

Figure 2.9   BOD Sources in Rio Negro

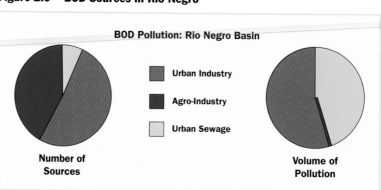

Source: CORNARE

Table 2.1   Pollution Charge Administration in Rio Negro

Sector	Total Pollution Sources	Sources Charged	Total Charges Assessed (Mill. Pesos)	Total Charge Payments (Mill. Pesos)
Urban Sewage	8	8	57.3	57.3
Urban Industry	55	43	65.6	64.4
Agro-Industry	46	41	.2	.2

Source: CORNARE

tion after the charges began had previously agreed to adopt cleaner technologies. Overall, although it is new, the Colombian experience provides support for the argument that a Baumol/Oates pollution charge system can work well in developing countries.

(2) Philippines

With a total surface area of about 90,000 hectares, Laguna Lake in Philippines is the second largest inland body of water in Southeast Asia. Twenty-one rivers flow into the lake, whose drainage region includes Manila and many smaller cities. According to the Laguna Lake Development Authority (LLDA), 1,481 factories occupied about 20 percent of the region's land area in 1994. While a few plants tap the lake's water for industrial cooling, most simply use the lake and its feeder streams as sinks for waste. Industry accounts for about 30 percent of the lake's pollution, while agriculture contributes about 40 percent and domestic sewage about 30 percent.

Philippines has long maintained a traditional regulatory system, and over 60 percent of local factories have adopted at least nominal pollution control. However, polluters had very little incentive to take regulators seriously because the inspection rate was low, legal enforcement was time consuming, and most ensuing fines were minimal. The results are evident in Figure 2.10, which summarizes a rigorous audit of water polluters before recent regulatory reforms. Only 8 percent of polluters were found to be in compliance.

To provide new incentives and restore Laguna Lake, the LLDA instituted an "environmental user fee" (EUF) for industrial pollution. Initial studies identified five industries as the primary sources of organic water pollution: food processing, hog farms, slaughterhouses, beverage firms, and textile makers. The agency first implemented pollution charges—in this case EUFs—in 1997, for a pilot group of 21 plants. The system has two parts: a fixed charge deter-

Figure 2.10   Results of Traditional Regulation

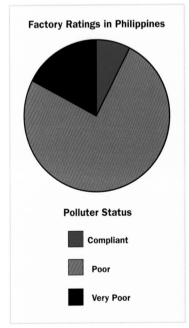

Factory Ratings in Philippines

Polluter Status

- ■ Compliant
- ▨ Poor
- ■ Very Poor

Source: DENR

41

mined by discharge volume, designed to cover administrative costs for LLDA, and a two-tier assessment for emissions. The latter includes one charge per unit of emissions that meet the legally permissible standard, and a higher unit charge for emissions above the standard. As in the Colombian case, abatement cost analyses provided the basis for setting charges at levels that would induce plant managers to cut pollution significantly.

After two years of implementation, LLDA reports that BOD discharges from the pilot plants have dropped 88 percent. Because pollution charges are remitted to LLDA, its resources for monitoring and enforcement have also increased significantly. In light of this experience, the Philippine Government has announced its intention to implement the EUF system nationwide.

Philippines' experience with pollution charges seems similar to that of Colombia in many respects. Faced with a continuous financial drain rather than sporadic legal action, plant managers have moved quickly to reduce pollution to the point where the marginal cost of abatement is equal to the pollution charge.

(3) Malaysia

During the 1960s and 1970s, Malaysia grew rapidly while diversifying exports away from its two traditional products, natural rubber and tin. The country selected palm oil for promotion, and by 1975 private palm oil plantations covered two-thirds as much area as private rubber estates (Figure 2.11). This economic boom, unfortunately, was accompanied by an environmental tragedy. Malaysia's palm oil mills discharged their waste effluent directly into nearby waterways. Since this discharge was laden with organic pollutants, the effect on aquatic life was catastrophic. Freshwater fish could no longer survive in 42 of Malaysia's rivers, marine spawning beds near river mouths were dying, and the stench from decomposing anaerobic waste was so bad that some riverside villages had to relocate.

Faced with this crisis, in 1974 the government passed the Environmental Quality Act and established the Department of the Environment (DOE), which could withhold operating licenses from severe polluters. This gave a strong, credible signal to the Malaysian palm oil producers, who began working on waste-treatment technologies. By mid-1977, the DOE was satisfied that the available technologies would support rapid pollution reduction at feasible cost.

The agency moved swiftly to enact a system that combined traditional regulations with pollution charges. Within four years, palm

Figure 2.11   Malaysian Palm Oil Plantation and Processing Mill

Source: Palm Oil Institute of Malaysia   *Source:* Malaysian Palm Oil Promotion Council   *Source:* Malaysian Palm Oil Promotion Council

oil mills were required to reduce BOD in their effluent from 5,000 parts per million (ppm) to 500 parts per million, with the understanding that the fourth-year standard would not be the final one. Operating licenses were issued for a flat M$100 fee, plus a charge of M$10 per ton of organic pollution discharged into water. Because the DOE had no way of valuing actual damages from pollution, it intended this charge to be high enough to provide some abatement incentive without being burdensome.

DOE added a surcharge of M$100 per ton for BOD discharges beyond the allowable limits. The surcharge, intended to have real teeth, was based on mandatory quarterly discharge reports verified by independent laboratories. Mills were required to apply for an operating license every year and include a description of their waste treatment system. DOE could reject license applications if it disapproved of the treatment approach—but it could also waive all fees for mills engaged in serious research and development on cost-effective pollution control.

In a single year, these combined measures produced a remarkable change: The mills' average daily discharges fell from about 220 tons to 125 tons. However, managers' decisions suggested that even the M$100 per ton surcharge was often below the marginal cost of abatement. Of 130 mills, 46 paid excess discharge fees of more than M$10,000, and 7 paid more than M$100,000. Compared with the compliance record in other countries, this was a good result; but full compliance with regulations should have lowered the average daily discharge to 25 tons, and the DOE professed disappointment. Now it faced a choice: It could retain the M$100 per ton surcharge while continuing to tighten the standard, raise the surcharge to induce faster compliance, or abandon the polluter-pays approach for stricter enforcement along traditional lines.

The Malaysian Government chose the third alternative. It abandoned the surcharge, maintaining only the M$10 per ton discharge fee, and specified that the standards would henceforth be mandatory. The agency proved its intent by taking legal action against many non-compliant mills during the ensuing years. And its approach worked. During the second year, the average mill reduced its BOD discharge to 60 tons. In two years, total organic pollution from Malaysia's palm oil mills fell from 15.9 to 2.6 million person-equivalents.[6] This occurred despite an increase in the number of mills from 131 to 147 and an increase in palm oil production from 1.8 to 2.6 million tons. By 1981, a sample survey suggested that 90 percent of the mills had cut BOD concentrations below 500 parts per million (ppm), and that 40 percent were below the sixth-year standard of 100 ppm. By 1991, 75 percent of the mills had dropped below 100 ppm, and organic pollution was less than 1 percent of its level when regulation began, even though palm oil production was at an all-time high.

To our knowledge, no study has attempted to separate the impacts of the fees, the legally imposed standards, and the waivers for R&D on abatement strategies. However, the regulatory package was clearly effective in reducing pollution and improving the quality of Malaysia's rivers. The estimated cost of compliance was also substantial—M$100 million by 1984—and in a highly competitive world market, palm growers bore most of the cost. However, the Malaysian boom absorbed this cost with no apparent problem. Unemployment remained low, and palm oil production remained profitable for most producers. Malaysia might have reached the same goal more cheaply by relying almost exclusively on pollution charges, since they would have allowed plant managers the freedom to minimize pollution-related costs. However, efficient enforcement of emissions standards got the job done in a country where public institutions have traditionally functioned very well.[7]

(4) China

In response to its serious emissions problems, China instituted pollution charges in 1979 (Figure 2.12), and almost all of China's counties and cities have implemented this system. Some 300,000 factories have paid for their emissions and more than 19 billion yuan have been collected. About 80 percent of these funds have been

Figure 2.12   Chinese Industry: Growing Pressure to Improve

Source: Curt Carnemark, World Bank   *Source:* Corbis

used to finance pollution prevention and control, accounting for about 15 percent of total investment in these activities.

In sheer magnitude, the Chinese charge system may be without peer in the world; it is also one of the few documented long-term applications of charges in a developing country. However, it differs greatly from an idealized charge system. Plants are charged only for pollution in excess of standards, and the charge is levied only on the single air or water pollutant that most seriously violates regulatory standards for each medium. The charges also provide insufficient economic incentives for compliance, since they are often too low to induce abatement to the legally required level.

China's regulators do impose serious penalties, including shutdowns, for plants that persistently violate standards, and have mandated that some large plants install abatement technologies. Charge revenues are earmarked to support regulators' budgets or pollution-control projects in the same region.

Although it has weaknesses, this system has proven highly potent in fighting pollution and cutting pollution intensity. For example, each 1 percent increase in the water pollution levy has led to a 0.8 percent drop in the intensity of organic water pollution from Chinese industry.[8] And each 1 percent rise in the air pollution levy has cut the pollution intensity of suspended particulates from industrial production by about 0.4 percent.[9]

The impact of these reductions during a period of rapid industrial growth has been remarkable. While industrial output has doubled, organic water pollution and air pollution have remained constant, and even declined in some areas. China's industrial pollution problem is far less serious than it would have been without the levies and other regulatory instruments.

China presents a paradox of success. According to estimates for cities like Zhengzhou and Beijing, the air pollution levy should be many times higher in China's major urban areas. But without the levy, pollution-related respiratory diseases would have seriously injured or killed hundreds of thousands more citizens.

China can build on this demonstrated success. For SEPA, the State Environmental Protection Agency, adjustment of the pollution levy is an important task for the next round of policy reform. The record of responsiveness so far suggests that as the levy rises, Chinese industry could reduce pollution far faster than anticipated.[10]

Lessons of Experience

The experiences of China, Philippines, and Colombia suggest that charges can generate a rapid, large, and sustained decline in industrial emissions. Charges appear to be an almost ideal tool because they provide maximum flexibility for both industry and regulators, who can use them to pursue varying levels of environmental quality.

Other significant lessons have also emerged.

(1) Flexible Enforcement

China's experience in using charges to control pollution shows that such charges generally flex with local circumstances. World Bank researchers recently investigated this experience in a collaborative project with SEPA. Using a new database on 29 Chinese provinces and urban regions from 1987 to 1993,[11] they compared actual water pollution charges collected with the amount of wastewater discharged in each region. They found that actual charges per unit of emissions vary widely, although the official rate is supposed to apply uniformly across China (Figure 2.13). This variation is not random: Charges are much higher in urbanized and industrialized provinces of the country, particularly the eastern coastal regions. Two factors explain these variations (Figure 2.14). The first is the price a community places on pollution damage, which varies with the total amount of pollution, the size of the exposed population, and local income per capita. The second is a community's capacity to understand and act on local environmental problems, which is influenced by its level of information, education, and bargaining power.

Figure 2.13   Pollution Charges in China

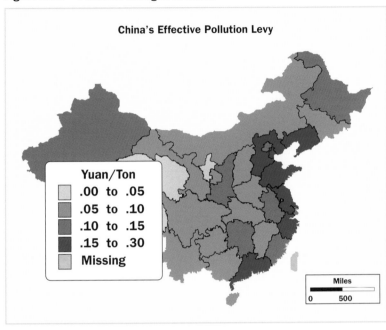

Source: Wang and Wheeler (1996)

Similarly determined variations in enforcement of emissions standards have appeared in other large countries such as Canada and India.[12] Both within and across countries, the available evidence suggests that enforcement varies systematically with local circumstances. Such community-level flexibility in administering national regulations is probably critical to continued support for either charges or standards in countries with highly varied environmental, social, and economic conditions.

(2) Building Support

Political realities indicate that industry has to support any charge system, and this support has proved contingent on four conditions. First, industry has to be convinced that the government is serious about environmental protection. Second, industrialists need credible evidence that pollution control will not bankrupt them. In both Philippines and Colombia, industry support gathered steam after numerous meetings in which regulators and international experts presented credible information about abatement costs. Third, plant managers tend to support charge systems once they under-

Figure 2.14   Why Provincial Levies Differ

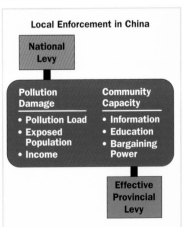

47

stand that these systems give them great flexibility. They can abate or pay, as their conditions warrant.

The fourth condition relates to how the charge revenues are used. Pollution charges are effective regulatory instruments because they reduce pollution through economic incentives. But while this argument appeals to economists, it cuts little ice with factory owners. To them, the charge is simply a tax—a financial sacrifice they have incurred for the common good. With remarkable consistency, they refuse to support charges until they are guaranteed that the revenues will be used to finance public or private waste-treatment projects in their own area. We will return to this issue in Chapter 6.

(3) Technical Foundations

To maintain a credible charge system, regulators must obtain reliable data on plant-level emissions. This requires the ability to audit emissions records, enter and store data, and analyze variations in effluent samples from each plant. Regulators also need good procedures for collecting and accounting for charge funds. These are stiff requirements, and many agencies are not capable of meeting all of them.

Some analysts have argued that information problems can be circumvented through the use of presumptive charges based on engineering estimates of pollution from plants of different kinds. In this system, regulators charge a plant using assumptions about the pollution intensity of its operations. The plant can either pay or reduce the charge by proving that its pollution is lower than the estimate. Presumptive charges have surface appeal because they seem to transfer monitoring costs to polluters, but regulators must still verify that emissions reports are correct, maintain consistent databases, and keep financial accounts. They are also saddled with the need to create and regularly update a large database of engineering parameters. And, of course, they inevitably have to deal with angry (and politically influential) factory owners who feel overcharged from the outset.

In practice, regulators are solving their information and auditing problems by using subcontractors rather than presumptive charges. In Colombia, for example, regulators rely on reports from bonded auditors to analyze emissions. The regulatory agency has also subcontracted fee collection and financial accounting to Colombia's largest commercial bank, which receives a fixed percentage of the revenue flow. This solution has a triple advantage: The bank has the right experience to operate such a system, it knows how to collect debts, and failure to pay these debts can threaten a firm's credit rating.

2.3 Targeting Enforcement

Despite the attractions of pollution charges, most countries still use traditional emissions standards to control air and water pollution. Yet rigid standards can inflict much economic harm if they are enforced without regard to benefits and costs. Fortunately, regulatory agencies can actually turn their inability to regulate all factories to their advantage by flexibly targeting plants for monitoring and enforcement.

Targeting can crudely approximate the results of a charge system by raising the expected penalties for large pollution sources with low abatement costs. And these plants will often respond more vigorously than other factories because they tend to have more skills to draw on, resources to buy and run complex equipment, and ability to spread their administrative costs over many units of activity.

Brazilian regulatory agencies have used such a targeting strategy to reduce pollution substantially while economizing on scarce administrative resources. The agencies assign factories to categories A, B, and C according to plant size, and target the largest (A) factories almost exclusively.

How effective is the ABC approach? A good illustration is provided by the case of FEEMA, the pollution control agency of Rio de Janeiro State. FEEMA program analysts have ranked several thousand factories according to their contribution to the overall volume and risks of local air and water pollution (Chapter 6). Figure 2.15 presents the results. Remarkably, the analysis suggests that 60 percent of the state's serious industrial pollution could be controlled by targeting only 50 factories in the A group. Controlling pollution from 150 plants in the B group would eliminate another 20 percent of the total. Targeting the first 300 plants in the C group, which numbers in the thousands, would cut 10 percent more pollution.

Targeting larger plants seems to have impressive potential for reducing pollution, but will it also save lives? Larger factories have taller stacks, so their emissions are more dispersed and less dangerous to nearby residents. But according to a recent study in Brazil (Box 2.2), large plants remain the source of most deaths because the sheer volume of their emissions simply overwhelms the higher per-unit hazard from smaller plants.

Figure 2.15 Polluters in Rio de Janeiro State, Brazil

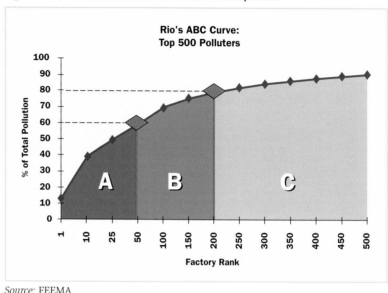

Source: FEEMA

The Brazilian pattern is not unique: Research in most countries and regions has revealed similarly skewed effects. The ABC approach can substantially reduce pollution by raising the marginal penalties for a few large polluters with relatively low marginal abatement costs. With enough information, regulators can further focus on plants whose abatement costs are exceptionally low, or whose pollution damage is exceptionally high.

2.4 Options for Policy Reform

Our case studies suggest that many roads can lead to reduced pollution. They also highlight flexibility as an important key to effective reform. Pollution charges work well because they provide economic incentives for cleanup while affording maximum flexibility to factory managers. Tradable pollution permit systems can provide similar advantages, although they have not been used as widely. Such systems fix overall pollution limits, and permit polluters to buy and sell rights to pollute within the overall limits. The United States has successfully used tradable permits to control national SO_2 emissions, and Chile has instituted a tradable permit system to control air pollution in Santiago. In the future, more developing countries may adopt tradable permit systems. At present, however, well-documented evidence on their implementation and impact remains scarce.

Box 2.2 Small Is . . . Bad or Beautiful?

Small enterprises have been controversial in the environmental and development literature. In *Small Is Beautiful,* E.F. Schumacher touted small plants as the agents of choice for sustainable development. Wilfred Beckerman responded with *Small Is Stupid,* which attacked the idea that small factories are environmentally benign. Beckerman argued that small factories are pollution-intensive, costly to regulate, and, in the aggregate, far more environmentally harmful than large enterprises. Recent reports from the World Bank and other international institutions have tended to side with Beckerman, but supporting data have been scarce.

Recently, a team from the Brazilian Census Bureau (IBGE) and the World Bank addressed this issue by estimating pollution-related deaths attributable to small, medium, and large factories in Brazil. The team combined an IBGE database of 156,000 factories with economic and demographic data from 3,500 Brazilian municipalities. To provide another interesting dimension, the team divided the municipalities into 10 groups according to per capita income.

The study estimated the impact of emissions on mortality in four steps:

- A standard World Bank model estimated the impact of emissions from small, medium, and large plants on the atmospheric concentration of particulates in each municipality.
- Ostro's "dose-response" function (Ostro, 1994) converted the estimated concentrations to mortality rates.
- Multiplication of mortality rates by municipality populations yielded expected numbers of deaths attributable to small, medium, and large plants.

Figure B2.2   Plant Size and Mortality in Brazil

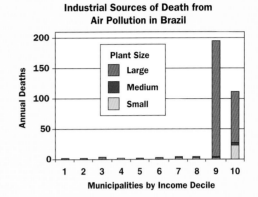

- Deaths were added across municipalities to obtain expected deaths by plant size for each income decile.

Figure B2.2 summarizes the results, which clearly show that large plants account for most industry-related air pollution deaths in Brazil. Most of these deaths occur in large urban areas such as São Paulo and Rio de Janeiro, whose municipalities are in the two highest income groups.

The IBGE-World Bank study concluded that some truth lies on both sides of the argument about small plants and pollution. Per unit of output, small plants pollute more and inflict more health damage than large plants. However, large plants dominate the mortality statistics because they produce far greater volumes of output and emissions. Since they also have much lower marginal abatement costs than small plants, they are a natural focus for ABC targeting by regulators with tight budgets.

Source: Dasgupta, Lucas, and Wheeler (1998)

Even under traditional standards-based regulation, ABC-style flexibility in targeting based on benefit-cost analysis can approximate the workings of a pollution charge system. Regional flexibility in enforcing national charges or standards also appears important for maintaining the support of communities with different environmental, social, and economic conditions.

In the next three chapters we will examine other effective roads to pollution control, including public disclosure of polluters' emissions and national economic reforms. Like pollution charges and targeted enforcement, these approaches reduce pollution by changing the calculations of plant managers who are trying to minimize pollution-related costs.

References

Baumol, W., and W. Oates, 1988, *The Theory of Environmental Policy* (Cambridge: Cambridge University Press).

Beckerman, W., 1995, *Small Is Stupid: Blowing the Whistle on the Green* (London: Duckworth Press).

Bressers, H., 1988, "The Impact of Effluent Charges: A Dutch Success Story," *Policy Studies Review,* Vol. 7, No. 3, 500–18.

Cohen, M., 1998, "Monitoring and Enforcement of Environmental Policy," Owen Graduate School of Management, Vanderbilt University, August.

Dasgupta, S., M. Huq, D. Wheeler, and C.H. Zhang, 1996, "Water Pollution Abatement by Chinese Industry: Cost Estimates and Policy Implications," World Bank Policy Research Department Working Paper, No. 1630, August.

Dasgupta, S., R. Lucas, and D. Wheeler, 1998, "Small Plants, Pollution and Poverty: Evidence from Mexico and Brazil," World Bank Development Research Group Working Paper, No. 2029, November.

Dasgupta, S., H. Wang, and D. Wheeler, 1997, "Surviving Success: Policy Reform and the Future of Industrial Pollution In China," World Bank Development Research Group Working Paper, No. 1856, November.

Dion, C., P. Lanoie, and B. Laplante, 1998, "Monitoring of Pollution Regulation: Do Local Conditions Matter?" *Journal of Regulatory Economics,* Vol. 13, No. 1, 15–8.

Jansen, H., 1991, "West European Experiences with Environmental Funds," Institute for Environmental Studies, The Hague, The Netherlands, January.

Ostro, B., 1994, "The Health Effects of Air Pollution: A Methodology with Applications to Jakarta," World Bank Policy Research Department Working Paper, No. 1301, May.

Pargal, S., M. Mani, and M. Huq, 1997, "Inspections and Emissions in India: Puzzling Survey Evidence on Industrial Water Pollution," World Bank Policy Research Department Working Paper, No. 1810, August.

Schumacher, E. F., 1973, *Small Is Beautiful: Economics As If People Mattered* (Reprinted in 1989 by HarperCollins, New York).

Vincent, J., 1993, "Reducing Effluent While Raising Affluence: Water Pollution Abatement in Malaysia," Harvard Institute for International Development, Spring.

Wang, H., and D. Wheeler, 1996, "Pricing Industrial Pollution in China: An Econometric Analysis of the Levy System," World Bank Policy Research Department Working Paper, No. 1644, September.

———— 1999, "China's Pollution Levy: An Analysis of Industry's Response," presented to the Association of Environmental and Resource Economists (AERE) Workshop, "Market-Based Instruments for Environmental Protection," John F. Kennedy School of Government, Harvard University, July 18–20.

End Notes

1. For a recent survey of the environmental economics literature on monitoring and enforcement, see Cohen (1998).

2. We use pollution per unit of output to reflect traditional pollution control laws. Environmental regulators do not expect a huge steel mill to produce the same pollution as a corner electroplating shop, but they do expect it to keep its pollution within feasible bounds. So traditional regulations generally focus on discharge intensity—pollution per unit of output or effluent volume—rather than discharge volume.

3. The estimated MSD graph for Zhengzhou slopes downward to the right, while the theoretical graph in Figure 2.2 slopes upward. This difference is caused by the mathematical form of the health impact model that researchers have created for Chinese cities. See Dasgupta, Wang, and Wheeler (1997) for further discussion.

4. The most recent edition is Baumol and Oates (1988).

5. Our thanks to our World Bank colleague Carl Bartone for detailed documentation of the Dutch pollution charge experience.

6. A person-equivalent is the amount of organic pollutant in the waste produced by one person in one year.

7. See Vincent (1993).

8. See Wang and Wheeler (1996).

9. See Wang and Wheeler (1999).

10. See Wang and Wheeler (1996); Dasgupta, Huq, Wheeler, and Zhang (1996).

11. See Wang and Wheeler (1996).

12. For evidence from Canada and India, respectively, see Dion, Lanoie, and Laplante (1998) and Pargal, Mani, and Huq (1997).

Development Dilemmas

Chapter Three

Communities, Markets, and Public Information

Sumatra, a huge island in the Indonesian archipelago, is home to the world's largest flower, Asia's largest volcanic lake, and indigenous peoples whose distinctive villages dot the volcanic highlands and forested lowlands. Sparsely populated and resource rich, Sumatra lies across narrow straits from Malaysia, Singapore, and the Indonesian island of Java. As their neighbors joined the East Asian miracle during the 1970s, the people of Sumatra found themselves squarely in the path of onrushing development. They stood their ground in a succession of conflicts over land use, resource exploitation, and environmental degradation. Some of these conflicts ended tragically, leaving social and environmental destruction in their wake. But some also ended happily, defining progressive new roles for government, business, and local communities.

The success story of PT Indah Kiat Pulp and Paper (IKPP) offers some insights into these new roles.[1] The largest pulp producer in Indonesia, IKPP is also the cleanest. Its mill at Tangerang, West Java, has received several national and international environmental awards, and its Sumatran mill at Perawang is fully compliant with national pollution regulations.

But IKPP wasn't always an environmental paragon. In 1984, its Sumatran operation began by importing an outdated factory from Taiwan (China) that employed elemental chlorine and discharged its wastes into the Siak River after minimal treatment. Round one of the mill's cleanup began in the early 1990s, with a backlash from local villagers. Allying themselves with local and national NGOs, the villagers claimed severe health damage from the mill's emissions and demanded more pollution control and compensation for their losses. In 1992 Indonesia's national pollution control agency, BAPEDAL, mediated an agreement in which IKPP acceded to the villagers' demands.

As this settlement was concluded, Indonesia's export boom ushered in round two for the mill. To finance a huge expansion in capacity, IKPP needed access to Western bond markets on favorable terms. Faced with potential concern in these markets over the company's long-term liability for pollution damage, IKPP managers opted to make a high-profile investment in clean production. The new facility uses world-class technology that is largely chlorine free and could be converted to totally chlorine-free production. IKPP has absorbed this technology easily because its parent corporation has a large, sophisticated engineering staff. What's more, IKPP has shown that large-scale clean production can be profitable in a developing country. Its performance has been so good that the company's stock value has increased while the Jakarta composite stock index has plunged 60 percent during the country's current financial crisis (Figure 3.1).

The PT Indah Kiat saga illustrates a new model for pollution control in developing countries. Formal regulation had little to do with pollution reduction at the Perawang mill. Defending their own interests, local communities applied pressure for cleanup and compensation. Abandoning the traditional agency role, BAPEDAL acted as a mediator rather than as a dictator of environmental standards. Later, pressure from international financial markets propelled IKPP to the next level of environmental performance.

In our basic terminology, local and international forces confronted IKPP with growing marginal expected penalties (MEP), even though government regulation was weak. Because it was a large branch facility of a sophisticated multiplant firm, the Perawang factory had relatively low marginal abatement costs (MAC). Faced with rapidly rising MEP and low MAC, IKPP's managers opted for a quick reduction in pollution intensity.

In this chapter we will argue that the forces that influenced IKPP—links among local communities, market agents, and regulators—have sparked several of the world's most innovative experiments in environmental policy in countries where traditional regulation has failed. These creative programs harness the power of public information, enabling communities and markets to exert maximum

Figure 3.1 Clean, Profitable Production

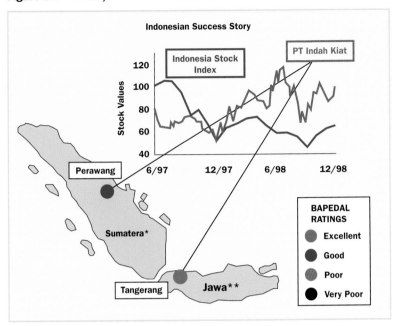

*English: Sumatra
**English: Java

influence on polluters. The results suggest that such pioneering efforts can have a significant impact on industrial pollution in developing countries.

3.1 Communities as Informal Regulators

Abundant evidence from Asia, Latin America, and North America shows that neighboring communities can strongly influence factories' environmental performance.[2] Where formal regulators are present, communities use the political process to influence the strictness of enforcement. Where regulators are absent or ineffective, NGOs and community groups—including religious institutions, social organizations, citizens' movements, and politicians—pursue informal regulation by pressuring polluters to conform to social norms (Figure 3.2). Although these groups vary from region to region, the pattern is similar everywhere: Factories negotiate directly with local actors in response to threats of social, political, or physical sanctions if they fail to compensate the community or reduce emissions.

Indeed, communities sometimes resort to extreme measures when sufficiently provoked. In the *Asian Survey*, Robert Cribb has

Figure 3.2   Communities and Polluters

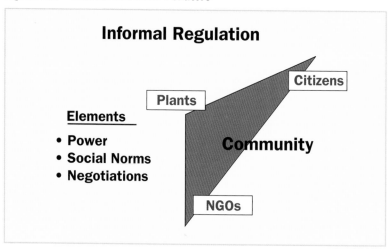

recounted an Indonesian incident "reported from Banjaran near Jakarta in 1980 when local farmers burned a government-owned chemical factory that had been polluting their irrigation channels." In a similar vein, Mark Clifford has reported in the *Far Eastern Economic Review* that community action prevented the opening of a chemical complex in Korea until appropriate pollution control equipment was installed.

When factories respond directly to communities, the results may bear little resemblance to the dictates of formal regulation. For example, Cribb also cites the case of a cement factory in Jakarta that—without admitting liability for the dust it generates—"compensates local people with an ex gratia payment of Rp. 5,000 and a tin of evaporated milk every month." In India, Anil Agarwal and colleagues (1982) describe a situation where, confronted by community complaints, a paper mill installed pollution abatement equipment—and, to compensate residents for remaining damage, the mill also constructed a Hindu temple.[3] If all else fails, community action can also trigger physical removal of the problem. In Rio de Janeiro, for example, a neighborhood association protest against a polluting tannery led managers to relocate it to the city's outskirts.[4]

3.2 The Power of the Market

The environmental concerns of market agents create additional incentives for pollution control (Figure 3.3). Green consumers are al-

Figure 3.3 Markets and Polluters

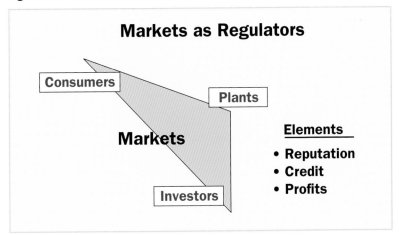

Several studies have confirmed that U.S. and Canadian stock markets react significantly to environmental news. Table 3.1 summarizes the evidence from recent studies, which report gains from good news and losses from bad news in the range of 1 to 2 percent. Do such changes actually motivate polluters to clean up? A recent study of toxic polluters by Konar and Cohen (1997) suggests that the answer is yes: Firms that experienced the greatest negative impact on stock prices reduced emissions the most.

To determine whether such forces affect firms in developing countries, World Bank researchers recently undertook a large-scale study of the impact of environmental news on stock prices in Argentina, Chile, Mexico, and Philippines. None of the four countries has a strong record of enforcing environmental regulations. Nevertheless, the study found that stock prices rise when authorities publicize good environmental performance and fall in response to public-

Table 3.1   Environmental News and Stock Values in Canada and the United States

Negative Performance Information	Impact on Stock Value
• Muoghalu et al. (1990)	Average loss of 1.2% (33.3 M $)
• Lanoie, Laplante (1994)	Average loss of 1.6% to 2%
• Klassen, McLaughlin (1996)	Average loss of 1.5% (390 M $)
• Hamilton (1995)	Average loss of 0.3% (4.1 M $)
• Lanoie, Laplante and Roy (1997)	Average loss of 2%
Positive Performance Information	
• Klassen, McLaughlin (1996)	Average increase of 0.82% (80 M $)

ity surrounding citizens' complaints.[5] In fact, the responses are much larger than those reported for U.S. and Canadian firms in Table 3.1: Gains average 20 percent in response to good news, and losses range from 4 to 15 percent in the wake of bad news. Figure 3.4 provides a striking illustration of such impacts for two firms operating in Philippines and Mexico. Overall, the message is clear: Capital markets

Figure 3.4   Environmental News and Stock Values in Philippines and Mexico

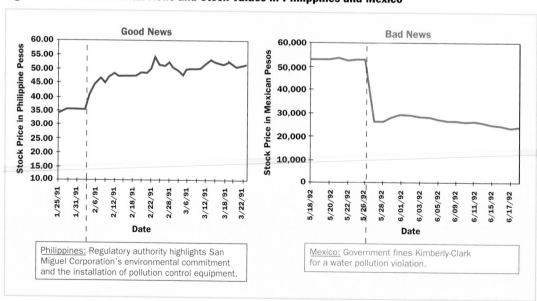

Source: Dasgupta, Laplante, and Mamingi (1997)

Figure 3.5   A Broader View of Regulation

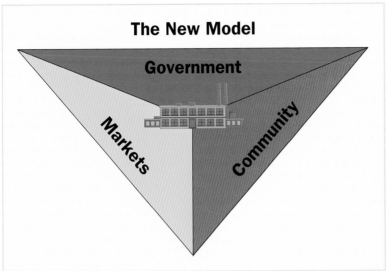

everywhere are taking information about environmental performance into account, and firms are responding by cleaning up.

Another powerful market influence has been exerted by the International Standards Organization through publication of ISO 14001, its most recent business performance standard. For the first time, this ISO standard includes explicit norms for environmental management. Hundreds of developing-country firms have already made the changes necessary to qualify for ISO 14001 certification. In Mexico, a recent study shows that even small enterprises seek ISO 14001 certification if they are interested in subcontracting relationships with large, ISO-certified enterprises (Chapter 4).

Once the roles of communities and markets are introduced, we have a much more robust model for explaining variations in polluters' behavior. Even where formal regulation is weak or absent, pressure applied through these new channels can significantly increase a plant's expected penalties for polluting. Polluters will react by reducing emissions, just as if government inspectors were enforcing regulatory standards.

This new story is captured by the regulatory triangle in Figure 3.5. Regulators still play an important part in controlling pollution, but their role is no longer confined to establishing and enforcing standards or charges. Instead, regulators gain leverage through programs designed to provide concrete information to communities and markets.

3.3 Getting PROPER in Indonesia

The story of a pioneering Indonesian program illustrates the new model in action. Starting in the 1980s, the Indonesian Government charged BAPEDAL, the national pollution control agency, with enforcing standards on discharges from industrial plants. But enforcement was weak because the regulatory budget was limited and the courts were plagued by corruption. Meanwhile industrial output was growing at over 10 percent annually. By the mid-1990s the government was becoming concerned about the risk of severe damage from pollution.

Faced with this predicament, BAPEDAL decided to initiate a program for rating and publicly disclosing the environmental performance of Indonesian factories. BAPEDAL hoped that the resulting pressure would provide a low-cost way to promote compliance with regulations, as well as create new incentives for managers to adopt cleaner technologies.

The program that ensued is called PROPER—for Program for Pollution Control, Evaluation and Rating.[6] Under PROPER, BAPEDAL rates each polluter on its environmental performance (Figure 3.6). Black denotes factories that have made no attempt to control pollution and are causing serious damage, while red denotes those that have instituted some pollution control but fall short of compliance. Factories that adhere to national standards receive a blue rating, and those whose emissions controls and production and waste-management procedures significantly exceed national standards receive a green label. World-class performers attain gold ranking.

In the pilot phase of PROPER, which began in early 1995, BAPEDAL rated water pollution from 187 plants. (The agency chose to concentrate on water pollution first because it had data and experience in that domain.) The pilot group included medium- and large-scale polluters from several river basins on the islands of Sumatra, Java, and Kalimantan. Initial ratings showed that two-thirds of the plants failed to comply with Indonesian regulations (Figure 3.7).

Although this showing was dismal by Western standards, fully one-third of the rated factories were in compliance despite BAPEDAL's evident inability to enforce regulations. The PT Indah Kiat saga suggests why: Two-thirds of the regulatory triangle—local communities

Figure 3.6   Rating Polluters in Indonesia

PERFORMANCE LEVELS	PROPER Ratings
GOLD	• **Clean technology, waste minimization, pollution prevention**
GREEN	• **Above standards & good maintenance, housekeeping**
BLUE	• **Efforts meet minimum standards**
RED	• **Efforts don't meet standards**
BLACK	• **No pollution control effort,** • **Serious environmental damage**

Figure 3.7   Before PROPER

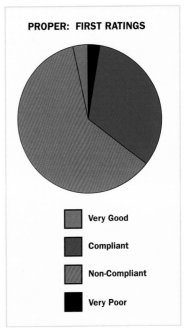

PROPER: FIRST RATINGS

- Very Good
- Compliant
- Non-Compliant
- Very Poor

Source: BAPEDAL

and markets—were already in place, albeit operating with poor information. These actors had already brought considerable pressure to bear.

Public disclosure is a political act and a media event, so BAPEDAL's leaders thought carefully about strategy before releasing the results. In June 1995, Indonesia's Vice President Tri Sutrisno presided over a high-profile public ceremony to congratulate the "good guys"—the five green-ranked plants whose performance exceeded formal requirements. After publicly rewarding these best actors, BAPEDAL privately notified other plants of their ratings, and gave the non-compliant ones six months to clean up before full public disclosure.

A scramble ensued as plants with red and black ratings considered their options, and by December striking changes had already occurred (Table 3.2, Figure 3.8). The most pronounced was a flight from the black group, which contracted by 50 percent. Red plants, on the other hand, felt less immediate pressure—only 6 percent im-

Table 3.2   PROPER's First Impact, 1995

	June	December	Change	% Change
Gold	0	0	0	0
Green	5	4	–1	–20
Blue	61	72	11	+18
Red	115	108	–7	–6
Black	6	3	–3	–50

Source: BAPEDAL

proved during the predisclosure period. One green plant also changed status, but not to gold: After the June announcement, the neighboring community had informed BAPEDAL that the plant was in fact polluting heavily under cover of darkness, and the facility was demoted to black. However, four of the original six black-rated plants improved their performance. This left three plants—the newcomer plus two laggards—in the black group by December. The net effect of these changes was an 18 percent expansion of the blue, or compliant, group. Even before public disclosure, PROPER had scored a considerable success.

In December 1995, BAPEDAL delivered on its commitment to full disclosure, releasing ratings by industry group over several months to hold media attention. By December 1996—one year later—improvements had become much more pronounced (Table 3.3, Figure 3.9). Compliant plants, originally one-third of the sample, now constituted over half. While the green group was unchanged, the blue group grew by 54 percent. Red-rated plants dropped by 24 percent, and the flight from black continued. Only one plant remained in the black category—a decline of 83 percent from the original size of that group.

Evidence from mid-1997 suggests that the program's strong impact has continued. For example, BAPEDAL's December 1995 ratings included 118 noncompliant factories—113 rated red and 5 rated black[7]—but by July 1997, 38 of those plants had achieved blue or green ranking (Figure 3.10). Only 18 months after full disclosure, PROPER had reduced pollution by more than 40 percent in the pilot group. Considerable turnover was evident in the lowest category: Four plants upgraded their ratings from black to red (3) or blue (1).

Figure 3.8   PROPER's First Impact

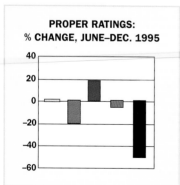

Source: BAPEDAL

Table 3.3 PROPER's Impact After 18 Months

	June 1995	December 1996	Change	% Change
Gold	0	0	0	0
Green	5	5	0	0
Blue	61	94	33	+54
Red	115	87	−28	−24
Black	6	1	−5	−83

Source: BAPEDAL

Four plants rated red in 1995 fell to black in mid-1997 as their condition changed or more information became available.

With continued political support, the PROPER team hopes to rate 2,000 plants annually by the year 2000. BAPEDAL has also been pursuing its own version of Brazil's ABC targeting strategy, so the share of total water pollution under PROPER's purview is much greater than the proportion of Indonesia's 20,000 factories that it rates (Figure 3.11). If PROPER extends to 2,000 factories within the next two years, it will cover about 10 percent of Indonesia's medium and large industrial plants but about 90 percent of total water pollution. As plant coverage expands, BAPEDAL intends to rate factories on air pollutants and toxic waste as well.

3.4 Evaluating PROPER

Given Indonesia's previous regulatory history, this remarkable result suggests that performance ratings and public disclosure can be powerful tools for improving environmental conditions in developing countries. Several factors have contributed to PROPER's success.

Public Disclosure and Pollution Control

Armed with PROPER-type performance ratings, citizens are in a much stronger position to negotiate pollution control agreements with neighboring factories. This is especially true because lack of information can distort communities' perceptions. For example, residents can often see or smell organic water pollution and sulfur oxide air pollution, but emissions of metals and toxins that accumulate in organisms' tissues are likely to escape notice. And even where pol-

Figure 3.9 Results of Disclosure

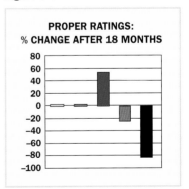

Source: BAPEDAL

Figure 3.10   Extended Impact

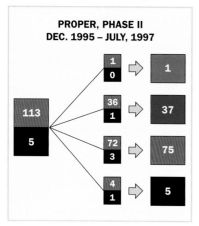

Source: BAPEDAL

lutants are clearly detectable, local communities may be unable to gauge the severity of their long-term impact or identify individual polluters. The PROPER system adds critical information to this picture and certifies the claims of local communities, which can use PROPER's ratings to engage the most serious polluters. PROPER also allows each community to more readily choose its own level of environmental quality.

Better information can also influence the market side of the triangle in Figure 3.5. Indonesia has a new stock market and, until the recent crisis, its rapidly expanding industrial economy has had extensive credit needs. With BAPEDAL's ratings, the stock market can more accurately value companies' environmental performance, and banks can factor pollution-related liability into their lending decisions.

For consumers, nothing less than a green or gold ranking may suffice, and the availability of information through outlets such as the Internet—which PROPER has used—may greatly influence their decisions.[8] All these factors should encourage polluters to clean up.

BAPEDAL itself benefits from public disclosure. More widespread adherence to environmental standards has boosted BAPEDAL's credibility with industry, NGOs, and the public and enhanced its ability to do its job. All regulators need good data about firms' pollution, but noncompliant firms have a clear incentive to withhold such information. Under PROPER, clean firms have an incentive to identify them-

Figure 3.11   PROPER's Expansion: "2000 by 2000"

PROPER'S EXPANSION PLANS

	Plants	Pollution
2000	2000	80%
1998	1000	60%
1996	400	40%
1995	187	20%

selves, and the agency can then home in on serious polluters and keep them in the public spotlight. Rewarding good performers also insulates regulators from charges that they are anti-business.

PROPER appealed to BAPEDAL because it had neither the resources nor the legal support to implement a traditional standards-based system. The agency's managers also decided that they lacked the capacity to enforce pollution charges. Viewing charge-based regulation as an inside transaction between the agency and a plant, they feared that corruption of their inspectors would distort emissions information and undermine the market-based approach. Public disclosure, by contrast, allows communities to check an agency's claims against their own daily experience.

PROPER bases its rankings on Indonesia's legal emissions standards, but disclosure systems could also use other benchmarks, such as the average intensity of emissions in each industrial sector or international performance standards. In fact, public disclosure does not have to rely on benchmarks at all—regulators could simply report each plant's emissions. The OECD's Pollutant Release and Transfer Register and the U.S. Toxics Release Inventory (Box 3.1) are examples of such disclosure programs.

However, in the developing world PROPER-type systems seem to be taking hold more rapidly. Their strength probably lies in two characteristics: They are compatible with standards-based regulations that are still on the books almost everywhere, and they rate environmental performance in a clear, straightforward format that is easy for the media to report and citizens to understand.

In principle, each locale could establish its own performance benchmarks to ensure maximum flexibility and efficiency. A sparsely populated area with few critical ecosystems, for example, could use laxer standards than a densely populated industrial area upstream from a marine sanctuary. A plant rated green in one area might well rate red in another. But neither the media nor political actors seem comfortable with such variations, and national and international market players and NGOs would find multiple-benchmark systems confusing.

Still, as we have seen, uniform performance standards can raise pollution control costs. To accommodate regional differences and enhance the efficiency of PROPER-type systems, national performance benchmarks might include three plant sizes, three levels of local environmental quality (heavy, medium, and light pollution), and vary according to industry sector.

Box 3.1 The U.S. Toxics Release Inventory

The U.S. Toxics Release Inventory (TRI) has annually reported polluters' emissions of more than 350 toxic chemicals for a decade. Since Congress established the program in 1986, TRI has published the names, locations, and toxic emissions—by chemical and medium of release—of plants with 10 or more employees that use at least 10,000 pounds of any listed chemical. The media and environmental groups provide extensive coverage of the yearly announcements. As the accompanying table shows, U.S. toxic emissions have declined substantially since TRI's beginning.

Programs like TRI use information differently from programs like PROPER. In the Indonesian case, a poor rating informs the public that a firm is not in compliance with national environmental standards. Disclosure programs such as TRI, by contrast, disseminate "raw" information on toxic emissions with no interpretation or risk assessment.

One problem is that some chemicals covered by TRI are quite dangerous, even in small doses, while others are hazardous only after long exposure at very high levels. By treating all chemicals the same, raw disclosure programs may sometimes alarm the public unnecessarily and pressure industry into adopting high-cost abatement programs that yield few social benefits. Academic researchers and NGOs have used media such as the Internet to inform the public of the relative risks of different chemicals, and to assist communities in identifying large polluters and assessing their overall pollution problems. (The Environmental Defense Fund maintains the most complete such Web site at *http://www.scorecard.org*.)

Community pressure is only one of several channels through which TRI exerts its effects; the financial community has also responded strongly. Research by Hamilton (1995) and Konar and Cohen (1997) has shown significant negative market returns for publicly traded firms when TRI first reports their pollution. Firms' market valuation also responds to information about changes in the volume of toxic pollution relative to toxic emissions from other firms. These results, in turn, create significant incentives to clean up: Firms with the largest

**Total Releases of TRI Chemicals
1988–1994 ('000 Metric Tons)**

	1988	1992	1993	1994	% Change 1988–1994
Total Air Emissions	1024	709	630	610	–40
Emissions to Surface Water	80	89	92	21	–73
Underground Injection	285	167	134	139	–51
On-Site Land Releases	218	149	125	128	–41
Total Releases	1607	1113	981	899	–44

stock market declines reduce emissions more than other firms. Numerous case studies have also shown that TRI induces firms to improve their ability to manage materials and waste.

These successes have inspired similar efforts in other countries, including the Chemical Release Inventory in the United Kingdom and OECD sponsorship of pilot Pollutant Release and Transfer Registers (PRTRs) in Egypt, the Czech Republic, and Mexico. The PRTR programs use the same format as TRI but restrict listed chemicals to those with relatively high hazard ratings.

The Costs of PROPER

PROPER's direct costs should include only those entailed in developing the ratings from existing information on emissions and disseminating the results. However, during the program's first 18 months, BAPEDAL devoted most of the program's resources to upgrading the agency's ability to collect and analyze data—efforts necessary for any effective pollution control program. The pilot program also employed foreign consultants, although PROPER has since operated with much lower levels of foreign involvement.

Despite these added expenses, PROPER's costs were only about $100,000 over the first 18 months. With 187 plants rated, the per-plant cost was $535, or $360 per year—just $1 per day. Given that this expenditure produced a 40 percent cut in organic water pollution, PROPER must be judged spectacularly cost-effective.

Of course, the acid test for the program comes after the international consultants have gone home and local industry realizes that life under PROPER will mean permanently increased pressure for pollution control. In Indonesia, the difficulties that normally accompany a program's adolescence have been compounded by the nation's severe economic crisis, which has produced dramatic cuts in BAPEDAL's budget. But paradoxically, the crisis seems to have strengthened PROPER's appeal. As resources for traditional monitoring and enforcement have diminished, Indonesia's leaders have found PROPER's low-cost leveraging of community and market action even more attractive.

Overall, PROPER-type programs are efficient because they leverage channels inaccessible to formal regulation. However, a recent study found that PROPER had a disproportionate impact on small factories, whose marginal abatement costs are typically high (Box 3.2). PROPER's effects also varied according to plant ownership: Reputation-sensitive multinationals responded most strongly, followed by private domestic firms, and then state enterprises. In short, PROPER induced factories of all types to cut pollution, but it shifted the relative burden to smaller plants and multinationals. The latter were relatively well positioned to bear this burden but the former probably were not. In the next chapter we will show how targeted efforts by government can help small factories overcome this disadvantage.

Implementing PROPER-Type Programs Outside Indonesia

When PROPER's impact first became apparent, other countries tempered their interest with a critical question: Since shame may be

Box 3.2 Changes in Compliance Patterns Under PROPER

Figure 3.7 summarizes initial compliance levels for the 187 factories in the pilot group for PROPER. A preliminary BAPEDAL/World Bank analysis of the program's impact has studied the effects of plant size, ownership (public, local, multinational), degree of export orientation, province, and industrial sector on compliance.

When PROPER began, plant size and public ownership had significant, positive associations with compliance; sectoral variations were also important, but multinational ownership had no effect. After 18 months, compliance patterns were very different. Plant size, public ownership, and sectoral variation had become insignificant as determinants of relative compliance. However, multinational ownership jumped to a very high level of positive significance while export orientation moved the other way—toward negative significance.

We interpret these results as follows. **Plant size**: Before PROPER, many big plants with low abatement costs had already reduced emissions because they faced significant expected pollution penalties from community and market action. Since smaller plants with higher abatement costs had not reduced pollution much in the "old regime," they found themselves in the spotlight once PROPER began. The resulting pressure forced them toward parity in compliance with big plants. **Ownership**: When PROPER began, publicly owned plants in Indonesia were more compliant than average.

This was unusual by international standards, since research on other countries has shown that such plants are normally heavy polluters (Chapter 5). However, after 18 months, the compliance status of publicly owned plants was not significantly different from the status of other domestically owned factories. The converse was true for multinational plants. Having started at parity in compliance with their domestic counterparts, they jumped to significantly higher compliance status. These results suggest highly varied sensitivity to environmental reputation: Multinationals are the most sensitive, followed by domestic private firms, and then state enterprises. PROPER increased pollution control in all three types of plants, but the strength of the response differed sharply. This result is consistent with the idea that public disclosure leverages pollution control through the operation of markets in which environmental performance is valued.

Finally, and paradoxically, the response to PROPER seems to have been perverse among more export-oriented plants. These factories responded more slowly than domestically oriented plants, so their relative (not absolute) compliance was lower after 18 months. This result suggests that different market channels have very different sensitivity to environmental information: International stockholders may be much more sensitive to environmental performance than international importers.

a strong motivator in a public disclosure program, does Indonesian culture make such a program particularly effective? The answer has proven to be no as other countries have begun PROPER-type programs.

The most advanced such effort is in Philippines, where the Department of Environment and Natural Resources (DENR) has created a program similar to PROPER, called EcoWatch. In April 1997 EcoWatch published its initial accounting for 52 factories in the Manila area. The summary showed that 48 plants ranked red or black, representing a 92 percent rate of non-compliance. As in Indonesia, the most compelling argument for public disclosure was the evident failure of the traditional approach (Figure 3.12).

To establish EcoWatch, the Philippine Government pursued a strategy similar to BAPEDAL's. President Fidel Ramos congratulated the blue plants in a public ceremony (there were no green or gold plants). Red and black plants were privately notified of their ratings and given a substantial period to reduce pollution. Full public disclosure occurred in November 1998, with broad media coverage. As in the Indonesian case, the program dramatically increased plants' compliance with national regulations. Although no factories reached green or gold status, blue ratings jumped from 8 percent in April 1997 to 58 percent in November 1998. Red ratings fell sharply, while black ratings remained almost constant.

Other countries are following closely in the wake of Indonesia and Philippines. Mexico is developing a program called Public Environmental Performance Indicators, or PEPI, and Colombia's public disclosure program will complement its pollution charge system. At least five other countries have also begun pilot implementation or active consideration of PROPER-type systems (Figure 3.13). What

Figure 3.12 Public Disclosure in Philippines

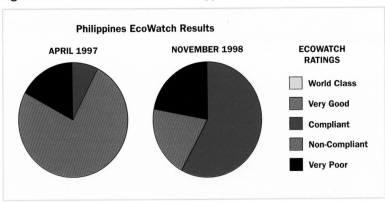

Source: DENR

Figure 3.13   PROPER's Legacy

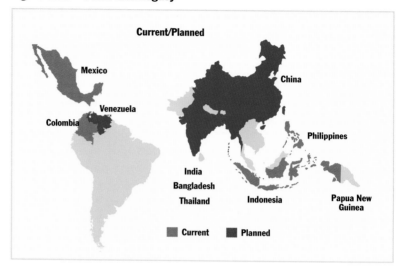

began as a ripple in Indonesia is clearly building into an international wave.

3.5 Regulating Pollution and Promoting Equity in the Information Age

Widespread acceptance of PROPER reflects a broader trend in public policy. Students of economic development are paying closer attention to the role of social capital—the informal relationships and institutions that strengthen developing communities. Similarly, legal scholars are focusing on the strong complementarity between social norms, which communities draw on to enforce public disclosure programs, and formal laws. The evidence shows that formal and informal regulatory mechanisms almost always coexist, but that the latter often dominate in developing countries where regulatory institutions are weak.[9]

In environmental policy, new thinking about the role of local influence reflects the insights of Nobel economist Ronald Coase, who called traditional regulation into question by noting that pollution victims, as well as regulators, can take action if they perceive that the benefits outweigh the costs.[10] As Coase noted, these costs stem from the need to acquire and analyze information, confront polluters, and negotiate settlements. Without good information such settlements may be far from optimal. Polluters and regulators usually have the most concrete knowledge of emissions; but polluters are unlikely to share this information in the absence of outside pressure, and bureaucratic inertia and/or legal constraints often prevent regulators from sharing information as well. Moreover, even if the public has information on emissions, it may not fully understand the risks it faces. Since polluters are also employers, good information on abatement costs is also important.

In short, effective local negotiations require good environmental information, and regulators will often be best positioned to supply it. They can play a valuable new role by focusing more resources on information collection and dissemination, including public disclosure of polluters. But a new role for regulators does not mean that they should abandon the traditional one. Efficient enforcement of regulations will remain very important—for its own sake, and because potential penalties provide an incentive for capital markets to react to public disclosure of non-compliance. In addition, as in the case of PT Indah Kiat in Sumatra, regulators can encourage local settlements by promoting negotiations, supplying the negotiators with objective information, and, as a last resort, posing the threat of official sanctions against non-compliant factories that refuse to negotiate with pollution victims.

Regulators can also serve the special environmental protection needs of poor communities. In countries as different as the United States, China, Brazil, and Indonesia, much of the variation in factories' environmental performance reflects the socioeconomic characteristics of the surrounding areas.[11] Local residents pressure polluters more successfully if they are richer, more educated, and better able to bargain because they have more employment options. In developed countries, the so-called NIMBY (not in my back yard) phenomenon stems largely from wealthy communities' ability to exclude polluting activities completely. Employment concerns may lead poor communities to welcome industrial activity, but such communities may lack enough political influence and environmental information to negotiate effective pollution control agreements. Economic development may be the best antidote to such problems in the long run, but in the meantime poor communities may suffer from excessive pollution.[12] Here environmental agencies can help, by educating communities on the pollution risks they face and ensuring that polluters conform to basic national norms. We will return to this issue in Chapter 4.

References

Afsah, S., B. Laplante, D. Shaman, and D. Wheeler, 1997, "Creating Incentives to Control Pollution," World Bank DEC Note, No. 31, July.

Afsah, S., B. Laplante, and D. Wheeler, 1997, "Regulation in the Information Age: Indonesia's Public Information Program For Environmental Management," World Bank, March.

Afsah, S., and J. Vincent, 1997, "Putting Pressure on Polluters: Indonesia's PROPER Program," A Case Study for the HIID 1997 Asia Environmental Economics Policy Seminar (Harvard Institute for International Development), March.

Agarwal, A., R. Chopra, and K. Sharma, 1982, "The State of India's Environment, 1982," New Delhi, India: Centre for Science and Environment.

Arora, S., and T. Cason, 1994, "Why do Firms Volunteer to Exceed Environmental Regulations? Understanding Participation in EPA's 33/50 Program," *Land Economics*, Vol. 72, No. 4, 413–32.

Clifford, M., 1990, "Kicking up a stink: South Korean Government reels from anti-pollution backlash," *Far Eastern Economic Review*, Oct. 18, 72–3.

Coase, R., 1960, "The Problem of Social Cost," *The Journal of Law and Economics*, Vol. 3, October, 1–44.

Cribb, R., 1990, "The Politics of Pollution Control in Indonesia," *Asian Survey*, Vol. 30, 1123–35.

Dasgupta, S., B. Laplante, and N. Mamingi, 1997, "Capital Market Responses to Environmental Performance in Developing Countries," World Bank Development Research Group Working Paper, No. 1909, October.

Dasgupta, S., R. Lucas, and D. Wheeler, 1998, "Small Manufacturing Plants, Pollution and Poverty: New Evidence from Brazil and Mexico," World Bank Development Research Group Working Paper, No. 2029, December.

Dasgupta, S., and D. Wheeler, 1996, "Citizen Complaints as Environmental Indicators: Evidence from China," World Bank Policy Research Department Working Paper, No. 1704, November.

Hamilton, J., 1995, "Pollution as News: Media and Stock Market Reactions to the Toxic Release Inventory Data," *Journal of Environmental Economics and Management*, Vol. 28, 98–103.

Hartman, R., M. Huq, and D. Wheeler, 1997, "Why Paper Mills Clean Up: Determinants of Pollution Abatement in Four Asian

Countries," World Bank Policy Research Department Working Paper, No. 1710, January.

Hettige, H., M. Huq, S. Pargal, and D. Wheeler, 1996, "Determinants of Pollution Abatement in Developing Countries: Evidence from South and Southeast Asia," *World Development*, Vol. 24, No. 12, 1891–904.

Hettige, H., S. Pargal, M. Singh, and D. Wheeler, 1997, "Formal and Informal Regulation of Industrial Pollution: Comparative Evidence from Indonesia and the US," *World Bank Economic Review*, Vol. 11, September.

Huq, M., and D. Wheeler, 1992, "Pollution Reduction Without Formal Regulation: Evidence from Bangladesh," World Bank Environment Department Working Paper, No. 1992-39.

Klassen, R., and C. McLaughlin, 1996, "The Impact of Environmental Management on Firm Performance," *Management Science*, Vol. 42, No. 8, 1199–214.

Konar, S., and M. Cohen, 1997, "Information as Regulation: The Effect of Community Right to Know Laws on Toxic Emissions," *Journal of Environmental Economics and Management,* Vol. 32, 109–24.

Lanoie, P., and B. Laplante, 1994, "The Market Response to Environmental Incidents in Canada: a Theoretical and Empirical Analysis," *Southern Economic Journal*, Vol. 60, 657–72.

Laplante, B., P. Lanoie, and M. Roy, 1997, "Can Capital Markets Create Incentives for Pollution Control?" World Bank Policy Research Department Working Paper, No. 1753, April.

Muoghalu, M., D. Robison, and J. Glascock, 1990, "Hazardous waste lawsuits, stockholder returns, and deterrence," *Southern Economic Journal*, Vol. 57, 357–70.

Pargal, S., and D. Wheeler, 1996, "Informal Regulation of Industrial Pollution in Developing Countries: Evidence From Indonesia," *Journal of Political Economy*, Vol. 104, No. 6, 1314 + .

Pfeiffer, S., 1998, "Power Plants Spark Protest; Blackstone Valley Residents Seek Halt," *Boston Globe*, Sept. 26.

Shane, P., and H. Spicer, 1983, "Market response to environmental information produced outside the firm," *The Accounting Review*, Vol. LVIII, 521–38.

Sonnenfeld, D., 1996, "Greening the Tiger? Social Movements' Influence on Adoption of Environmental Technologies in the Pulp and Paper Industries of Australia, Indonesia and Thailand," Ph. D. Thesis, University of California, Santa Cruz, September.

Stotz, E., 1991, "Luta Pela Saude Ambiental: A AMAP Contra Cortume Carioca, S. A., Una Experiencia Vitoriosa," V. V. Valla and E. N. Stotz (eds.), *Participacao Popular, Educacao e Saude*, Rio de Janeiro, 133–60.

Tietenberg, T., and D. Wheeler, 1998, "Empowering the Community: Information Strategies for Pollution Control," paper presented at the conference "Frontiers of Environmental Economics," Airlie House, Virginia, Oct. 23–25.

Wang, H., and D. Wheeler, 1996, "Pricing Industrial Pollution In China: An Econometric Analysis of the Levy System," World Bank Policy Research Department Working Paper, No. 1644, September.

End Notes

1. For a detailed account, see Sonnenfeld (1996).

2. See Pargal and Wheeler (1996), Hettige, Huq, Pargal, and Wheeler (1996), Huq and Wheeler (1992), Hartman, Huq, and Wheeler (1997), and Dasgupta, Lucas, and Wheeler (1998).

3. Such arrangements are not confined to developing countries. Even in strictly regulated societies like the United States, communities can make life difficult for plants that violate local norms, whether or not their activities meet formal regulatory requirements. A good example is the recent controversy over proposed construction of four new electric power plants in Massachusetts' Blackstone Valley. Although the proposed plants easily exceed regulatory requirements—and indeed, they have been lauded by environmental groups—the plants have met with stiff community resistance. Local leaders have protested that three power plants already operate in the region, and that four more facilities will harm the community's quality of life, use up water, and lower property values. According to Sacha Pfeiffer (1998), writing in the *Boston Globe*, "In order to make the plants 'more palatable,' several power companies have offered compensation packages to Blackstone Valley communities, including money for high school scholarships, new water and sewer facilities and water conservation programs."

4. See Stotz (1991).

5. See Dasgupta, Laplante, and Mamingi (1997).

6. For detailed descriptions and analyses of PROPER, see Afsah, Laplante, Shaman, and Wheeler (1997), Afsah, Laplante, and Wheeler (1997), and Afsah and Vincent (1997).

7. During the predisclosure period, PROPER rated several additional plants, finding two new blacks and five new reds. Red and black plants therefore number 118 in Figure 3.10 and 111 in Table 3.2.

8. BAPEDAL's PROPER ratings can be found on the agency's Web site: *http://www.bapedal.go.id/profil/program/proper.html.*

9. For a more detailed discussion, see Tietenberg and Wheeler (1998).

10. See Coase (1960).

11. See Pargal and Wheeler (1996), Hettige, Pargal, Singh, and Wheeler (1997), Hettige, Huq, Pargal, and Wheeler (1996), Huq and Wheeler (1992), Hartman, Huq, and Wheeler (1997), and Dasgupta, Lucas, and Wheeler (1998).

12. See Dasgupta and Wheeler (1996), Wang and Wheeler (1996), and Pargal and Wheeler (1996).

Paso del Norte Ozone Map
Healthy   Unhealthy

El Paso
Juárez

Industrial Dualism, Poverty, and Pollution

Source: *Corbis*

Chapter Four

Knowledge, Poverty, and Pollution

Mexico's border with the United States runs from the Pacific Ocean to the Rio Grande, then winds southeast with the river until it empties into the Gulf of Mexico near Matamoros. Along this 1,900-mile frontier, thousands of *maquiladora* factories assemble products for duty-free export to the United States. Their explosive growth has provided employment for thousands of young Mexicans, but some factories have also contributed to pollution along both sides of the border.

Some of the worst pollution problems occur in the Paso del Norte region, where the Rio Grande crosses from the United States into Mexico. Here the cities of Ciudad Juárez, Mexico, and El Paso, Texas, flank the river in a high desert valley that is prone to thermal inversions. In the 1980s, air pollution mounted as growth in both cities accelerated. The U.S. Environmental Protection Agency cited El Paso's air quality as substandard, and U.S. environmental groups opposed to the North American Free Trade Agreement (NAFTA) pointed to the region's problems. Better to defer NAFTA, some argued, until Mexican industry could handle pollution problems like those in the Paso del Norte.

But which "Mexican industry"? Some firms handle their pollution problems very well. Cemex (Cementos Mexicanos), for example, operates cement plants all over Mexico while setting a world standard for environmental performance.[1] Cemex's Barrientos facility was the first cement plant in the Americas to receive ISO 14001 certification, and Mexico's Environment Ministry has publicly lauded six Cemex plants for their participation in a voluntary environmental audit program.

In the border region, some maquiladora plants are undoubtedly serious polluters. But many specialize in garment and electronics assembly operations that are less pollution intensive than heavy manufacturing. For example, in 1997 about 80 percent of maquiladora factories were assembly operations (garments, electrical equipment, furniture, auto parts, etc.), 15 percent were in general manufacturing, and 5 percent produced chemicals.[2]

In fact, the worst industrial pollution in Juárez has no direct link to NAFTA or maquiladora production.[3] It comes from small brick kilns, which belch filthy smoke from combustion of scrap wood, old tires, used motor oil, and sawdust laden with toxics (Figure 4.1). The kilns evoke Mexico's historic poverty, not its new prosperity. Most brick makers live near their work sites in cardboard or scrap wood shanties, in which families crowd five to a room. Some 40 percent of the households report the death of at least one child. Even the kiln owners average only three years of schooling, and a quarter are illiterate.

Originally isolated in outlying squatter settlements, the kilns were absorbed by urban sprawl as Juárez expanded. They posed numerous air pollution hazards for their neighbors, principally from fine particles and carbon monoxide but also from volatile organic compounds, nitrogen oxide, sulfur dioxide, and heavy metals.[4] As public awareness of such hazards grew, kiln-related incidents became the largest source of community complaints to the Ciudad Juárez environmental authority.

Technically, the solution was clear: replace scrap fuels with propane or natural gas. However, fierce price competition prevented fuel switching in the crude brick market. Rapid bankruptcy loomed for any kiln operator who used propane, which cost 28 percent more than scrap fuels despite state subsidies. Switching fuels also entailed acquiring a new burner, learning how to use it, and modifying the kiln itself.

Traditional regulation provided little incentive to switch. The local environmental authority was not only understaffed but reluctant to confront the brick makers, many of whom were allied with politically powerful organizations. Some 40 percent belonged to an affiliate of the Partido Revolucionario Institucional (PRI), Mexico's dominant political party. Another 19 percent, in the poorest *colonias*, belonged to the Comite de Defensa Popular (CDP), which had formed to resist the political establishment's attempts to evict squat-

Figure 4.1   Fuel Use and Pollution from Kilns

Two Options for Firing Bricks

Smoke from Scrap Fuel

The Clean Option: Gas Firing

Source: Corbis; Courtesy of Octavio Chavez, Southwest Center for Environmental Research and Policy (SCERP), Instituto Tecnologico y de Estudios Superiores de Monterrey — Campus Ciudad Juarez (ITEMS), and Salud y Desarrollo Comunitario de Ciudad Juarez (SADEC/FEMAP)

ters. This tradition of resistance affected attitudes toward the local environmental agency, based partly on the fear that pollution control would bankrupt the kilns and eliminate jobs for over 2,000 of the poorest people in Juárez.

Public pressure finally broke the regulatory deadlock in the early 1990s. Action was sparked by election of a new municipal president, whose mandate included strong action to reduce pollution from the kilns. He banned dirty fuels and routinely jailed or fined violators. Support came from local and national NGOs, led by the Mexican Federation of Private Community Health and Development Associations (FEMAP). FEMAP and the city authorities launched an aggressive public campaign to educate the brick makers and their neighbors about the health risks from burning scrap. In private meetings, they persuaded the brick makers' organizations to support conversion to propane. Sensing an important business opportunity, local propane suppliers offered the kiln owners free equipment to encourage fuel-switching. Engineers from local universities provided free technical assistance, and engineers from the El Paso Natural Gas Company suggested more efficient kiln designs.

Paradoxically, the controversy over NAFTA also encouraged rapid progress, as transborder pollution became an important pawn in the struggle for public opinion. Anxious to promote the free-trade agreement, the U.S. Government offered technical support for the switch to propane. Motivated partly by NAFTA and partly by rising public interest in pollution control, the Mexican Government and its local PRI affiliate tacitly supported the municipal president's campaign against kiln-based pollution.

From 1990 to 1992, these forces converged to transform small-scale brick making in Juárez. Over half of the city's 300 brick makers switched to propane firing, and pollution from the kilns dropped sharply. This transformation resonated far beyond Juárez, as it demonstrated the feasibility of pollution control by small-scale industry in the informal economy. However, the triumph was short-lived, as Mexico began eliminating subsidies for basic commodities such as propane under its economic reform program. From 1992 to 1995, the 28 percent cost differential between propane and scrap firing leaped to 162 percent.

Bankruptcies and unemployment loomed as the remaining scrap-fired kilns easily undercut their cleaner competitors, and this seismic shock destroyed the community consensus that had supported conversion to propane. As support from community groups and brick makers' organizations evaporated and the municipal government dropped its punitive enforcement stance, the clean kilns quickly retreated to scrap firing.

Still, community awareness of pollution damage remained, with residents redirecting their efforts into formal and informal pressures to discourage use of the dirtiest scrap fuels—tires, battery cases, and used motor oil. A positive response from many brick makers has kept emissions below their 1990 level, albeit higher than the level after propane conversion.

The Ciudad Juárez story illustrates two ways that public action can reduce industrial pollution. First, environmental education and political mobilization can lead local communities to raise marginal expected pollution penalties (MEP; Figure 4.2). In Juárez, the community fought pollution through formal channels, by filing complaints against the kilns and electing a municipal president who

Figure 4.2   Mexican Brick Makers in the '90s: MAC vs. MEP

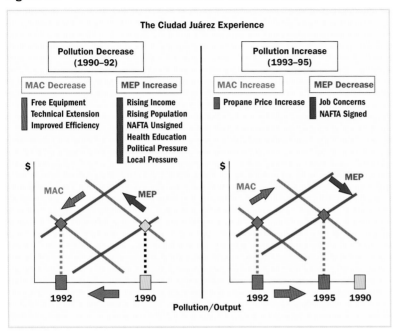

tightened enforcement. Informally, community-based NGOs pressured the brick makers' organizations to support conversion to propane. Reversal occurred when national decontrol of propane prices raised marginal abatement costs (MAC) again, but MEP didn't revert to its 1990 level because environmental awareness had grown.

Governments can also cut pollution by providing support for conversion to clean production, thereby lowering marginal abatement costs. This approach is a promising alternative to traditional regulation because it wields a carrot rather than a stick. It may also reduce pollution more cheaply than enforcement of formal regulations, which requires monitoring, data analysis, and, if necessary, police action—all time-consuming and expensive ways to raise MEP.

However, many economists have maintained that public intervention to curb pollution should stop at the factory gate, for a simple and sensible reason: Factory managers know their operations better than regulators, who should simply establish incentives. When CETESB, São Paulo's pollution control authority, launched an aggressive campaign to reduce pollution of the Tiete River, program managers attributed over 50 percent of the improvement to changes in manufacturing processes rather than installation of pollution control equipment.[5] Environmental agencies do not typically promote such changes directly.

This arm's-length regulatory model works effectively when well-informed factory managers can easily revamp their technology as incentives shift. But what happens when plant managers face high conversion costs with little certainty about outcomes? One response might be that fast learners will adjust and expand while others will suffer losses and leave the business. This approach has surface appeal, but it didn't survive the test of experience in Ciudad Juárez, as concern for jobs prompted the community to assist many kiln owners in taking the initial steps toward cleaner production.

Polluters often must make even more fundamental changes in the way they do business to curb emissions. Is technical assistance useful and feasible in more complex situations? An affirmative response requires credible evidence that changes in plant management can significantly reduce pollution, and that governments can help firms make the needed changes at affordable cost. Recent research from Mexico suggests that developing countries can satisfy both conditions.

4.1 Helping Firms Adopt Environmental Management

Certification by the International Standards Organization (ISO) offers one vehicle for pursuing such initiatives. The ISO certifies international auditing firms, which in turn scrutinize the quality of factories' processes according to ISO guidelines. ISO-certified businesses, especially those seeking rapid growth in the international marketplace, enjoy a competitive advantage because they can assure potential customers that they maintain high quality standards. Many leading firms prefer subcontractors that have satisfied ISO requirements.

The latest benchmark, ISO 14001, includes new standards for environmental management systems (EMS) based on thousands of firm-level case histories. According to this benchmark, plants must take the following EMS steps to achieve ISO certification:

- Perform an initial managerial review to identify environmental issues of concern, such as excessive use of polluting inputs and the potential for a serious environmental accident;
- Establish priorities for action, taking into account factors such as local environmental regulations and potential costs;
- Establish an environmental policy statement, signed by the CEO, that includes commitments to compliance with environ-

mental regulations, pollution prevention, and continuous improvement;

- Develop performance targets based on the policy statement (such as reduction of emissions by a set amount over a defined period);
- Implement the environmental management system (EMS) with defined procedures and responsibilities; and
- Measure performance and conduct management audits.

Since the ISO published the preliminary version of 14001 in 1996, factories in both developed and developing countries have rushed to obtain certification. Some 8,000 plants achieved certification by January 1999.[6] Asia leads other developing regions, but Latin America has also seen significant activity, and three African countries (Egypt, Morocco, and South Africa) are represented (Figure 4.3,

Figure 4.3   International Diffusion of ISO 14001

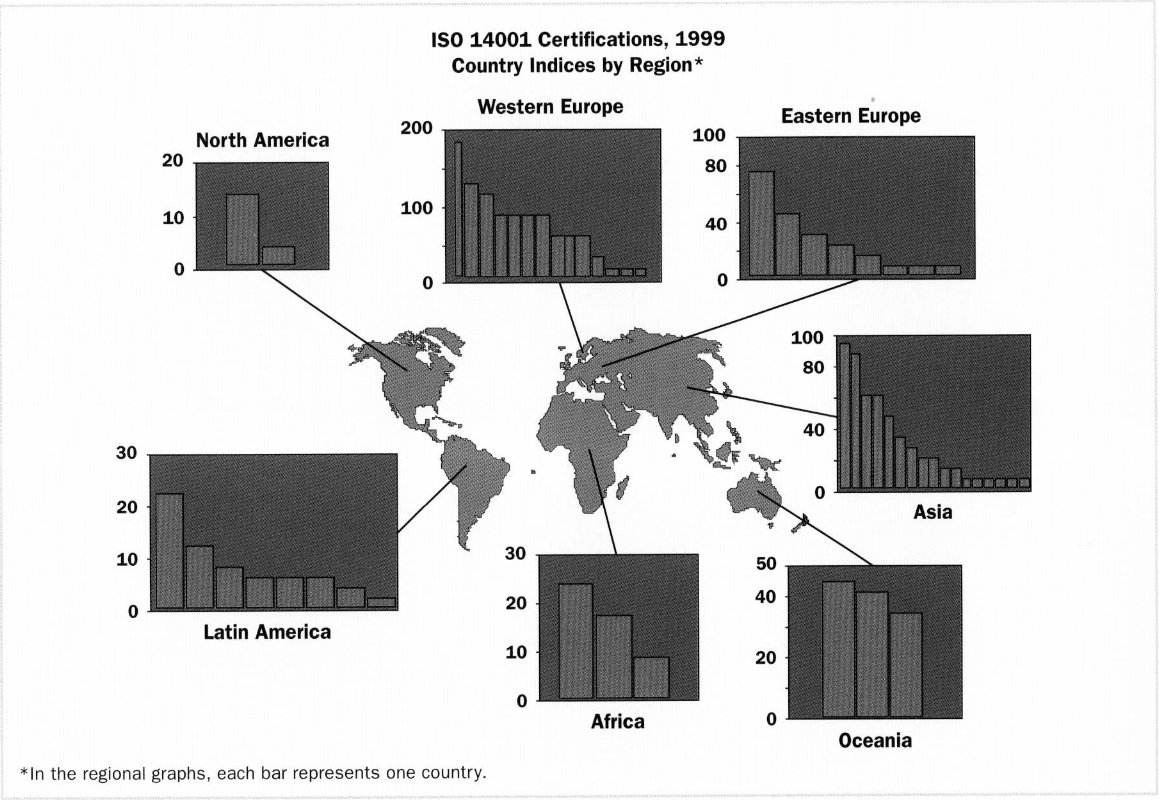

ISO 14001 Certifications, 1999
Country Indices by Region*

*In the regional graphs, each bar represents one country.

Source: ISO World

Table 4.2).[7] The developed world is split: Western Europe and Japan lead in certifications, while the United States and Canada lag behind many newly industrialized countries that depend heavily on international trade.

A recent World Bank study examined a large sample of Mexican factories to determine whether factories that adopt ISO 14001 procedures reduce pollution (Box 4.1).[8] Almost 50 percent of these factories had adopted few or no procedures necessary for ISO certification, while 18 percent had completed most or all of the required steps (Table 4.1). The research shows that process is important: Plants that have completed most of the ISO 14001 steps comply with pollution regulations far more than plants that have completed few steps.[9]

We also investigated the degree of "environmental mainstreaming": whether the plants had assigned environmental responsibilities to general managers rather than specialized managers, and whether the plants provided environmental training for all workers as well as environmental personnel. The plants varied substantially in their adoption of such practices (Table 4.3). But our research shows that mainstreaming works: Providing environmental training for all plant personnel and assigning environmental tasks to general managers help plants comply with regulations.

Large vs. Small Plants

The Mexico survey suggests that targeting assistance to help smaller plants adopt such procedures would yield the biggest payoff. That's partly because large factories are much better equipped to monitor their own pollution (Figure 4.4). The survey shows that only 5 percent of large plants lacked that capacity. Some 60 percent of small plants could not monitor their air pollution or hazardous waste, while 40 percent lacked the ability to monitor water pollution.[10]

Differences in plant size also affect the rate at which plants adopt ISO-type EMS procedures. Large branch plants with well-educated workers score 70 points higher on our EMS adoption index (Table 4.1) than small, individually owned plants operating with lower-skilled labor.

The Mexico study reveals the consequences of these variations for environmental performance: The regulatory compliance rate is only about 25 percent for small, individually owned plants such as the brick kilns of Ciudad Juárez, whose workers have little education (Figure 4.5). By contrast, the compliance rate is over 70 percent

Box 4.1 Environmental Management and Regulatory Compliance in Mexico

To learn more about the role of environmental management in promoting compliance with pollution regulations, the World Bank participated in a survey of Mexican industry with a team of regulators, academics, and industrialists.[11] This team conducted confidential interviews at 236 representative factories in all size classes for four key polluting sectors: food, chemicals, nonmetallic minerals, and metals.

Figure B4.1a shows that about half of the factories regularly fail to comply with Mexican regulations. The study investigated the relationship between compliance and four measures of plant-level environmental management: (1) percent completion of steps like those necessary for ISO 14001 EMS certification, (2) assignment of personnel to environmental tasks, (3) assignment of environmental

Figure B4.1b   EMS and Compliance

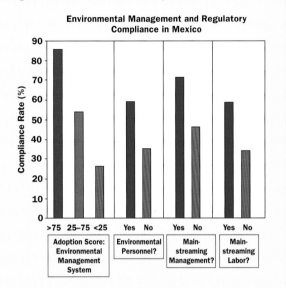

Source: Dasgupta, Hettige, and Wheeler (1997)

tasks to general managers rather than use of specialized managers, and (4) environmental training for workers other than specialized personnel.

The results (Figure B4.1b) highlight the importance of environmental management and training, particularly the adoption of ISO 14001-type procedures. Some 86 percent of plants with high EMS adoption scores comply with regulations, while only 24 percent of plants with low scores comply. Plants that have assigned personnel to environmental tasks report much higher compliance than others (58 percent vs. 34 percent), as do plants that have mainstreamed environmental concerns among managers (71 percent vs. 47 percent) and workers (59 percent vs. 34 percent).

Figure B4.1a   Mexican Polluters

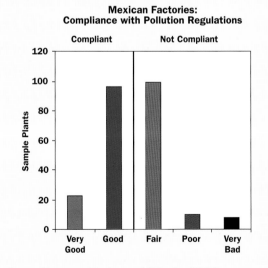

Source: Dasgupta, Hettige, and Wheeler (1997)

Table 4.1   Adoption Index for ISO 14001 Procedures by Mexican Factories

Adoption Score	Number of Plants	Percent
S ≤ 25	111	47.0
25 < S ≤ 50	45	19.1
50 < S ≤ 75	38	16.1
75 < S ≤ 100	42	17.8

Source: Dasgupta, Hettige, and Wheeler (1997)

Table 4.2   ISO 14001 Certification, 1999 by Country and Region

Region/ Country	Number Certified	Index* Value	Region/ Country	Number Certified	Index* Value	Region/ Country	Number Certified	Index* Value
Africa			**Latin America**			**W. Europe**		
Egypt	15	21	Costa Rica	2	22	Denmark	300	175
South Africa	21	16	Argentina	37	12	Sweden	400	172
Morocco	2	6	Brazil	65	8	Ireland	80	121
Asia			Mexico	27	8	Finland	130	105
			Chile	4	6	Switzerland	292	93
Korea	463	95	Uruguay	1	5	Austria	180	80
Malaysia	80	82	Colombia	3	4	UK	950	78
Thailand	100	59	Peru	1	2	The Netherlands	300	75
Singapore	60	59	**E. Europe**			Germany	1100	47
Japan	1542	32				Belgium	120	45
Philippines	23	26	Hungary	31	69	Norway	60	38
Hong Kong	40	24	Slovak Rep.	8	40	Spain	116	20
Turkey	40	20	Slovenia	6	31	France	177	12
Indonesia	43	19	Czech Rep.	12	22	Italy	100	9
India	60	16	Croatia	3	15	Portugal	7	7
China	60	7	Poland	8	6	Greece	6	5
Pakistan	2	3	Rumania	1	3	**North America**		
Oceania			Russia	1	1			
Mauritius	2	47				Canada	90	15
New Zealand	27	45				USA	210	3
Australia	130	34						

* Index = (Number Certified)/GDP, standardized to the range 1–200.

Table 4.3   Mainstreaming Environmental Management in Mexican Factories

Management strategy	Yes	%	No	%
Environmental training for nonenvironmental workers?	76	32.6	157	67.4
Environment manager also has other responsibilities?	211	93.8	14	6.2

Source: Dasgupta, Hettige, and Wheeler (1997)

for large branch plants of publicly traded firms, which employ many workers with secondary-school education. As Figure 4.5 shows, plant size, firm size and worker education contribute roughly equally to compliance.

Since many large plants already have EMS capability, government promotion of environmental management should focus on small- and medium-scale enterprises (SMEs). But from a public policy perspective, doing so makes sense only if SMEs actually adopt EMS procedures, and if such intervention reduces pollution more cheaply than conventional regulation. For evidence on this issue, we turn to another recent Mexican project.

Figure 4.4   Plant Size and Monitoring Capacity

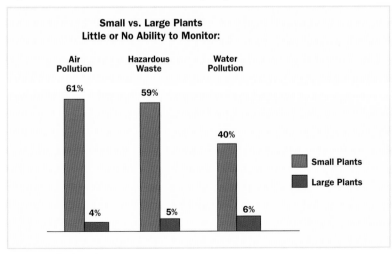

Source: Wells (1996)

Figure 4.5   Plant Size and Compliance in Mexico

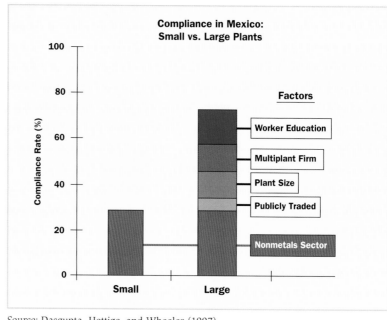

Source: Dasgupta, Hettige, and Wheeler (1997)

Lessons from Guadalajara

Monitored experiments in promoting EMS within plants remain rare; one notable exception is a recent project in Guadalajara, Mexico, that tested whether SMEs could successfully adopt environmental management systems. Eleven large companies, many of them multinationals, agreed to provide assistance to 22 small- and medium-scale suppliers who were interested in improving their environmental performance. The project, which enlisted the private sector, local academic institutions, the Mexican Government, and the World Bank, entailed several two-month cycles of intensive training, implementation, and review sessions.[12]

After nine months of implementation, the 15 SMEs remaining in the project rated their degree of EMS adoption on a 20-point scale. In May 1997, the average adoption score was effectively zero. By February 1998, average scores had increased to around 16 points for environmental planning and 11 points for EMS implementation. About 80 percent of the plants reported lower pollution, and nearly 50 percent reported improved compliance and waste handling. Many also reported improved work environments, more efficient use of materials, and better overall economic performance (Figure 4.6).

Figure 4.6   Results From Adoption of ISO 14001

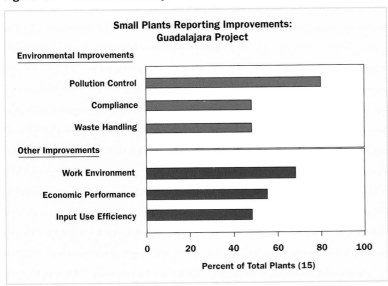

Source: Ahmed, Martin, and Davis (1998)

The Guadalajara project showed that SMEs can successfully adopt EMS—with assistance. These plants will probably sustain the changes, because the project covered the fixed costs of adjusting to an environmental management system; the incremental costs of operating an EMS should be much lower. Participating SMEs have also altered their internal communications to provide constant feedback on environmental problems and solutions. Once formed, this new business culture will not easily disappear.

The Guadalajara project reduced pollution by lowering marginal abatement costs (MAC) rather than raising marginal expected pollution penalties, as in conventional regulation. The evidence suggests that this alternative approach was cost competitive. The project's total cost was around $200,000. Because about 10 plants realized significant benefits, the unit cost was approximately $20,000 per plant.[13] To compare the project (an investment) with conventional regulation (an annual flow of costs), we use the discounting approach. We employ a 10 percent discount rate and assume that a reduction in MAC from EMS adoption is sustainable. This yields an annualized cost of $2,000 per factory in perpetuity.

To estimate the cost of future projects in Guadalajara, we assume that local consultant fees are about 25 percent of fees charged by the international consultants in the pilot program. The implied unit cost is $5,000 per plant, or $500 in annualized costs—roughly equivalent to a month's wages for a skilled worker in urban Mexico. To achieve similar results each year, conventional regulation would almost certainly require equal or greater time and costs devoted to monitoring, record keeping, and enforcement. What's more, traditional regulation is less likely to yield the economic benefits of EMS stemming from greater overall efficiency. We conclude that promoting EMS among SMEs compares favorably with attempting to regulate these enterprises by conventional means.

Because they have been monitored and evaluated systematically, both the Ciudad Juárez project and the Guadalajara project provide important new information about the power of government-supported learning to reduce pollution by SMEs. The Ciudad Juárez project revealed the feasibility of improving pollution control in informal-sector, low-technology enterprises operated by some of urban Mexico's poorest, least-educated workers. Farther south, the Guadalajara project showed the feasibility of encouraging EMS adoption by somewhat more sophisticated small- and medium-scale subcontractors to large firms. In both Ciudad Juárez and Guadalajara, project funds financed the development of local consulting skills that will contribute to future pollution-reduction initiatives in the private sector.

4.2 Who's Complaining about Pollution?

In Ciudad Juárez, effective regulation required feedback to kiln owners from the surrounding community. This is not an isolated case. Despite their putative independence, pollution control agencies respond to the demands of the political institutions that determine their budgets and, ultimately, their legitimacy. Political leaders, in turn, respond to citizen complaints from communities affected by pollution.

Regulators also have an administrative reason to heed community protests: Monitoring is costly and agencies' budgets are lean in developing countries, so they cannot remain fully informed about all polluters. As a result, regulators often focus resources on responding to citizen complaints. For example, the pollution control agency of Brazil's Rio de Janeiro State devotes nearly 100 percent of its inspection resources to complaints. After setting aside 50 percent of its resources for targeting priority polluters, São Paulo's pollution control agency allocates the remainder to complaints. In Indonesia, the na-

areas, which are also likely to be areas where industry concentrates. Cheaper housing and industrial job opportunities give the poor a double incentive to locate in more polluted areas, even if they are fully informed about health risks.

Social, political, and historical factors have generated severe income inequality in many developing regions. Yet where poverty is the root cause of pollution exposure, invoking environmental injustice can backfire. Suppose, for example, that a movement against environmental injustice targets a large polluting factory located in the middle of a poor residential area. Neighboring families are well aware of the pollution, but they have located there because rents are cheap and the factory offers jobs for semiskilled workers. The environmental justice movement succeeds, and the plant's managers reduce pollution by shifting to a process that uses preassembled components and requires more educated labor. The air and water in the surrounding neighborhood become noticeably cleaner, and pollution-related illnesses fall.[21]

After the victory celebrations, however, other changes occur. Because the area is much cleaner, land values and rents rise. The poorest residents have little choice but to pack their belongings and move, since they can no longer afford shelter in the area. Their job opportunities also decline, because the factory no longer needs much semiskilled labor. Some of their neighbors accept the higher rents, but they have to find new jobs in other parts of the city. To continue working, they spend more hours jammed into buses and other vehicles, risking their lives on congested, polluted roads. In the aftermath of the movement's supposed success, its intended beneficiaries are worse off, because it has confused an income-inequality problem with environmental injustice.

What, then, is environmental injustice? In our view, two different concepts are well worth considering. First, the government could assume responsibility for maintaining a minimum decent standard of environmental quality for all citizens. This would resemble a public commitment to universal primary education. Failure to maintain the minimum decent standard would be defined as environmental injustice, warranting corrective action. This would include conventional pollution regulation, but could also mean programs that promote access to safe water and basic sanitation for poor communities.

A second concept would apply where people suffer from pollution because of ignorance as well as poverty. Governments should provide environmental education to all communities, so failure to inform poor neighborhoods about dangerous pollution would qualify as injustice. The Ciudad Juárez case shows how effective public education can be. Very poor people in the *colonias* supported regulation of the kilns after an education campaign persuaded them that the health benefits would compensate for the additional risk of unemployment and higher rents. The program worked because it targeted serious polluters and provided assistance for their conversion to propane firing. Better-informed *colonias* continued to support cleaner production after propane price decontrol, but concern for jobs shifted their focus to pressure for cleaner scrap fuels.

Ciudad Juárez demonstrated the power of public education to promote environmental change even when poverty remains unaltered. In our view, this is an important arena in which the struggle for environmental justice should be joined.

References

Afsah, S., B. Laplante, and D. Wheeler, 1997, "Regulation in the Information Age: Indonesian Public Information Program For Environmental Management," World Bank, March.

Ahmed, K., P. Martin, and S. Davis, 1998, "Mexico: The Guadalajara Environmental Management Project," World Bank, September.

Blackman, A., and G. Bannister, 1998a, "Pollution Control in the Informal Sector: The Ciudad Juárez Brickmakers' Project," *Natural Resources Journal*, Vol. 37, No. 4, 829–56.

———, 1998b, "Community Pressure and Clean Technology in the Informal Sector: An Econometric Analysis of the Adoption of Propane by Traditional Mexican Brickmakers," *Journal of Environmental Economics and Management*, Vol. 35, No. 1, 1–21.

Chávez, O., 1995, "Alternative Fuels for Brick-Makers, CD Juárez, Mexico Project," Southwest Center for Environmental Research and Policy (SCERP). Reproduced from the SCERP Web site at *http://www.civil.utah.edu/scerp/brickmaker/brickmaking.html.*

Dasgupta, S., H. Hettige, and D. Wheeler, 1997, "What Improves Environmental Performance? Evidence from Mexican Industry," World Bank Development Research Group Working Paper, No. 1877, December.

Dasgupta, S., R. Lucas, and D. Wheeler, 1998, "Small Plants, Pollution and Poverty: Evidence from Mexico and Brazil," World Bank Development Research Group Working Paper, No. 2029, November.

Dasgupta, S., H. Wang, and D. Wheeler, 1997, "Surviving Success: Policy Reform and the Future of Industrial Pollution in China," World Bank Policy Research Department Working Paper, No. 1856, October.

Dasgupta, S., and D. Wheeler, 1996, "Citizen Complaints As Environmental Indicators: Evidence From China," World Bank Policy Research Department Working Paper, No. 1704, November.

Hamson, D., 1996, "Reducing Emissions from Brick Kilns in Ciudad Juárez: Three Approaches," Border Environment Research Reports, No. 2, Southwest Center for Environmental Research and Policy (SCERP), June. Reproduced from the SCERP Web site at *http://www.civil.utah.edu/scerp/docs/berr2.html.*

Hartman, R., M. Huq, and D. Wheeler, 1997, "Why Paper Mills Clean Up: Determinants of Pollution Abatement in Four Asian Countries," World Bank Policy Research Department Working Paper, No. 1710, January.

Hettige, H., M. Huq, S. Pargal, and D. Wheeler, 1996, "Determinants of Pollution Abatement in Developing Countries: Evidence from South and Southeast Asia," *World Development,* Vol. 24, No. 12, 1891–1904.

Ostro, B., 1994, "The Health Effects of Air Pollution: A Methodology With Applications to Jakarta," World Bank Policy Research Department Working Paper, No. 1301, May.

Pargal., S., M. Huq, and M. Mani, 1997, "Inspections and Emissions in India: Puzzling Survey Evidence on Industrial Water Pollution," World Bank Development Research Group Working Paper, No. 1810, August.

Pargal, S., and D. Wheeler, 1996, "Informal Regulation of Industrial Pollution in Developing Countries: Evidence From Indonesia," *Journal of Political Economy*, Vol. 104, No. 6, 1314 +.

Petzinger, T., 1996, "Mexican Cement Firm Decides to Mix Chaos into Company Strategy," *Wall Street Journal*, December 13.

Stotz, E., 1991, "Luta Pela Saude Ambiental: A AMAP Contra Cortume Carioca, S.A., Una Experiencia Vitoriosa," V. V. Valla and E. N. Stotz (eds.) *Participacao Popular, Educacao e Saude,* Rio de Janeiro, 133–60.

Wang, H., and D. Wheeler, 1996, "Pricing Industrial Pollution in China: An Econometric Analysis of the Levy System," World Bank Policy Research Department Working Paper, No. 1644, September.

—— 1999, "China's Pollution Levy: An Analysis of Industry's Response," presented to the Association of Environmental and Resource Economists (AERE) Workshop, "Market-Based Instruments for Environmental Protection," John F. Kennedy School of Government, Harvard University, July 18–20.

Wells, R., 1996, "Prevención y Control de la Contaminación en la Industria Mexicana: Reporte de Una Encuesta," (Lexington, Mass: The Lexington Group), December.

End Notes

1. See Petzinger (1996) for a report on Cemex's innovative role in Mexican business.

2. Statistics reported by Mexico's Secretariat for Commerce and Industrial Promotion (SECOFI) at *http://www.nafta-mexico.org/export.htm.*

3. Our discussion of the Ciudad Juárez case draws heavily on two papers by Allen Blackman and Geoffrey Bannister (1998a,b), which document the authors' extensive primary research and econometric analysis. Our thanks to Allen Blackman for additional discussion of Ciudad Juárez in a series of personal communications. For additional information about the brick kiln pollution problem, see Hamson (1996) and Chávez (1995).

4. Blackman and Bannister (1998a) cite a study of brick makers in Saltillo, Mexico, that finds that 47 percent of subjects tested had "abnormal" pulmonary functions. See Ostro (1994) for detailed discussion of the impacts on health of particulates.

5. Interviews with CETESB staff.

6. Reinhard Peglau of the Federal Environmental Agency, Republic of Germany, provided these estimates. They are reproduced by ISO World at *http://www.ecology.or.jp/isoworld/english/analy14k.htm.*

7. To control for extreme scale differences, such as between Costa Rica and China, we divided each country's total certifications by its GDP, and standardized the result on a scale from 1 to 200.

8. See Dasgupta, Hettige, and Wheeler (1997).

9. The study recognizes the possibility of reverse causation: Once other factors have convinced plant managers to comply with regulations, they could implement the ISO 14001 steps as part of the improvement process. However, this would not imply that the ISO 14001 steps caused the improvement. The research (Dasgupta, Hettige, and Wheeler, 1997) uses standard econometric techniques to adjust for this problem.

10. See Wells (1997).

11. Participants included Mexico's National Environment Ministry (SEMARNAP), the Monterrey Institute of Technology, and the Mexican National Association of Industries. Both the survey questionnaire and the data are available online at *http://www.worldbank.org/nipr/work_paper/1877/survey/index.htm.*

12. This summary is based on a World Bank report by Ahmed, Martin, and Davis (1998).

13. The final project report estimates the cost of the pilot project to be $135,000, excluding the time and travel costs of World Bank staff. Including these factors would increase the estimated cost to around $200,000.

A second approach would apportion the cost among all 15 participating plants, lowering the apparent cost per plant. However, measured benefits were apparently zero for 5 plants, so this approach would yield the same result as the first, because the expected value of results per plant would be lowered proportionately.

14. Complaint-response systems in Brazil, China, and Indonesia are familiar to the authors from collaborative work with FEEMA, CETESB, BAPEDAL, and China's State Environmental Protection Agency (SEPA).

15. See Dasgupta and Wheeler (1996). Data linking environmental conditions, pollution complaints, and community characteristics in China are available online at *http://www.worldbank.org/nipr/data/china/status.htm #Province.*

16. See Wang and Wheeler (1999).

17. See Wang and Wheeler (1996) and Dasgupta, Wang, and Wheeler (1997).

18. See Pargal, Huq, and Mani (1997) and Hartman, Huq, and Wheeler (1997).

19. See Dasgupta, Lucas, and Wheeler (1998) and Pargal and Wheeler (1996).

20. See Dasgupta, Lucas, and Wheeler (1998).

21. In extreme cases, the targeted plant may simply move away. Stotz (1991) describes such a case for a tannery in Rio de Janeiro, Brazil. Environmental regulators in Rio have reported to the authors that middle-income residents led the movement against the plant; lower-income families were far more reluctant to act, because they valued the tannery as a source of employment.

Outside and Inside Cubatao: Brazil's Serra do Mar in the 1980s

Source: *Carlos Renato Fernandes and Eco Parana; Corbis*

Chapter Five

National Economic Policies: Pollution's Hidden Half

Southeast of São Paulo, Brazil's continental plateau crests in the Serra do Mar before dropping off sharply to the sea. Along the crest stand remnants of Brazil's fabled Atlantic Forest, one of the world's most diverse and threatened ecosystems. As the highway from São Paulo winds down the coastal scarp to Santos, the region's major seaport, it encounters a small, quiet river. Upstream and surrounded on three sides by mountains lies the industrial city of Cubatao. In the 1980s it was known as the "Valley of Death."

In the go-go days of Brazil's state-led development, the valley's location made it irresistible to industrial planners. Near the port of Santos, it was a perfect place for industries like steel, petroleum, fertilizer, and chemicals to turn imported heavy raw materials into finished products before shipping them to São Paulo via the long climb uphill. The river provided a source of water as well as a convenient place to dump wastes.

Led by huge state corporations like COSIPA (steel) and PETROBRAS (oil), the Cubatao valley mushroomed into an industrial complex so large that it accounted for 3 percent of Brazil's GDP by 1985. Employment boomed for immigrants from Brazil's poor regions, and the future looked bright—except for two unfortunate lapses by nature. The small, quiet-flowing river was no match for the torrent of industrial wastewater, and the valley was a natural trap for air pollution. Undeterred by local regulators, state-owned mills and their private counterparts spewed a thousand tons of pollutants into the air every day. In the early 1980s the city recorded the highest infant mortality rate in Brazil, and over one-third of the residents suffered from pneumonia, tuberculosis, emphysema, and other respiratory sicknesses. By 1984, the Cubatao River was basically dead from organic pollution. Downstream from Cubatao, tons of heavy metals accumulated in bottom sediments and washed into the sea near Santos. Above the valley, fallout from air pollution began killing the Atlantic Forest and denuding the mountainsides.

Finally, in January 1985 the crisis became a catastrophe, as 15 inches of rain poured onto the bare hillsides in 48 hours. Hundreds of mudslides cascaded into the valley, and one broke a large ammonia pipeline in Vila Parisi, releasing gas that injured many residents and forced a mass evacuation. Official denial ended as the governor of São Paulo State declared an emergency and mandated forceful action by CETESB, the state's pollution control agency.[1]

Fifteen years later much has changed in the Cubatao Valley. It is still no paradise, but environmental conditions are typical of medium-sized industrial cities in Brazil. The Atlantic Forest is growing back, sunny days are a reality again, children are healthier, and fish are returning to the Cubatao River, although their tissues are still laced with toxic metals. CETESB deserves great credit for this restoration. Supported by an aroused populace, its actions have made air pollution emergencies rare and cut damaging emissions considerably (Figure 5.1).[2]

Only one obstacle prevented even faster cleanup—the resistance of the state-owned factories that spearheaded the valley's development. By 1994, state enterprises contributed 42 percent of total suspended particulates (TSP) before end-of-pipe control but 77 percent of the actual emissions after control (Figure 5.2). The case of sulfur dioxide (SO_2) was similar. State-owned factories were simply doing far less to abate pollution than private mills. Even this substandard performance had required years of targeted inspections by CETESB, embarrassing public disclosures, and shutdown threats. Managers of the state-owned plants stubbornly resisted, complaining about financial losses and invoking political support at the state and national levels.

Things changed abruptly in late 1993 when the government privatized COSIPA, the state-owned steel company. The Cubatao plant shared in the industry's ensuing rapid modernization. From 1990 to 1996, Brazilian steel mills expanded production from 22.6 to 25.2 million tons while doubling output per worker.[3] Use of materials is

Figure 5.1   Air Pollution, 1984–1998

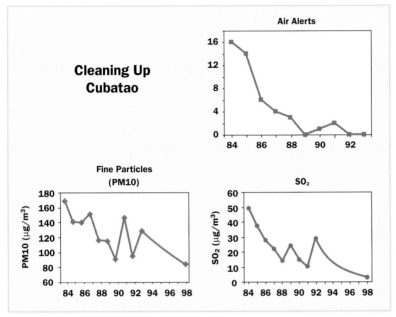

Source: CETESB

down, quality is up, and there is widespread interest in the new ISO 14001 quality standard, including its environmental provisions. CETESB also finds it easier to regulate the privatized Cubatao steel mill. Although Brazil's privatization program had no explicit environmental goals, it proved to be a godsend for hard-pressed pollution control agencies like CETESB.

The impact of privatization on Cubatao is not an isolated case: National economic policies affect industrial emissions so strongly that they constitute "pollution's hidden half." Recent research shows that cleaner production generally results from economic reforms— reducing barriers to international trade, privatizing state industries, developing new stock markets, eliminating subsidies for energy and raw materials, and deregulating domestic industries. However, such reform is not a panacea. Few countries reform their economies for environmental reasons, so it would be a peculiar stroke of luck if all such actions had clean impacts. In some cases economic reform can actually increase industry's pollution intensity, and the faster growth sparked by more-open markets magnifies the potential for pollution.

Fortunately, numerous studies have suggested ways to anticipate and offset such side effects while economic reform attacks pol-

Figure 5.2   Ownership and Pollution

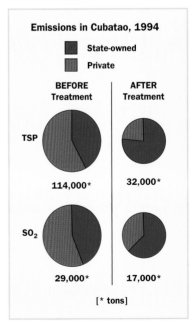

Source: CETESB

lution's "hidden half" on a broad front. Incomes should also rise with economic reform, increasing public support for formal and informal regulation of pollution. However, ensuring lower pollution requires close cooperation between economic reformers and environmentalists, as well as added resources to help regulators monitor pollution in the wake of reform.

5.1 How Trade Reform Influences Polluters

When developing countries become more "open"—cutting tariffs and lowering other barriers to international trade—domestic firms have better access to cleaner manufacturing technologies. Such technologies emerged rapidly in the 1970s because of stricter environmental regulation in the OECD economies.[4] In steel making, for example, continuous casting revolutionized production by eliminating energy-intensive intermediate stages, thereby reducing pollution by about 20 percent. The use of electric arc furnaces in the industry also grew rapidly, partly because the process is far less pollution-intensive. In the paper industry, thermomechanical pulping greatly reduced the need for polluting chemicals.

Although these new technologies were available on world markets soon after they were developed, weak regulation in developing countries provided little incentive for plants to adopt them for environmental reasons. However, the new technologies also operated more efficiently than their predecessors. Lowering trade barriers made them cheaper to acquire, and potentially increased domestic firms' interest in more efficient production by opening the market to international competition.

To determine whether open developing economies absorbed these technologies more rapidly than closed economies, a World Bank research team examined steel and paper production in 50 countries. We found that the open economies led closed economies in adoption of cleaner technologies by wide margins (Figure 5.3), and that the open economies reaped significant environmental benefits. For example, we estimated that more rapid adoption of continuous casting and electric arc technology made steel making in the open economies about 17 percent less pollution-intensive than in the closed economies.[5]

Some economists have also argued that greater openness to trade can encourage cleaner manufacturing because protectionist countries tend to shelter pollution-intensive heavy industries. In the early 1990s, a World Bank team found that pollution intensity was indeed higher in protectionist Latin American economies than in

Figure 5.3 Trade Policy and Adoption of Clean Technology

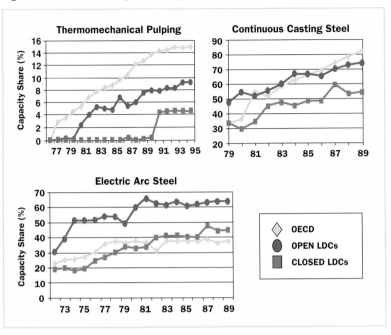

Source: Wheeler, Huq, and Martin (1993)

countries with fewer barriers to trade. Another Bank team uncovered the same result in a study encompassing all developing countries.[6] Recent evidence from China suggests that greater openness to trade has reduced the share of dirty sectors (Box 5.3).

However, research at the plant level in Indonesia, India, and Mexico has found that factories with more external trade links do not have lower pollution intensity, nor are they more likely to comply with environmental regulations.[7] Thus, we can conclude that countries that are more open to trade adopt cleaner technologies more quickly, but individual factories that are export oriented have no special advantage. Open economies also seem to harbor fewer pollution-intensive industries.

Of course, growing international trade may stimulate more production, swamping cuts in pollution intensity and raising a country's total pollution. We will address that problem later in the chapter.

5.2 How Input Prices Affect Pollution

Eliminating subsidies for energy and raw materials, and breaking up protected monopolies that produce them, change the prices of these goods. Because industry relies heavily on such inputs, changes in their prices also exert significant effects on industrial pollution—sometimes in opposing directions.

Much previous research, for example, suggests that materials-intensive industries also produce a lot of waste. Thus, eliminating subsidies for raw materials—thereby raising their prices—shifts production toward processes that use fewer materials and pollute less. (End-of-pipe pollution control also uses material inputs such as chemicals. Increasing their cost makes end-of-pipe control more expensive and thus less likely to be used. Overall pollution declines, however, because process-level waste reduction more than compensates for the end-of-pipe effect.)[8] On the other hand, breaking up monopoly producers of raw materials should increase competition and reduce prices. Companies should respond by using more materials, thereby increasing pollution intensity.

Cutting energy subsidies has opposing effects at the plant and industry levels. Several research projects have shown that raising energy prices also tends to raise pollution intensity *for individual plants* (Box 5.1).[9] Higher energy prices increase the cost of end-of-pipe treatment, thereby discouraging pollution control. They also induce substitution away from relatively clean, capital- and energy-intensive processes that generate fewer waste residuals. Electric arc furnaces and thermomechanical pulping are examples of such processes.

However, raising energy prices tends to lower pollution intensity *for industry as a whole* because sectors that process heavy raw materials (and generate most of the pollution) are also heavy energy users. As energy becomes more expensive, demand shifts toward products that are less energy (and pollution) intensive. Higher energy prices also reduce energy demand, lowering production from power plants that are often heavy air polluters. The conventional assumption is that these industry-level effects are greater than countervailing plant-level effects, so higher energy prices should reduce overall pollution from industry. However, data scarcity has prevented careful research on this issue in developing countries. Even if the overall impact of higher energy prices is beneficial, some local areas may suffer from greater pollution if local factories become much more emissions intensive. In Ciudad Juárez, the impact of propane price decontrol on brick-kiln emissions provided an excellent case in point.

Figure 5.4 illustrates possible responses to economic reforms at a plant whose managers minimize costs by equating marginal abate-

Box 5.1 Beyond Anecdotes: Building a Database through Collaborative Research

Information scarcity makes research on industry-and-environment issues difficult in developing countries. National and regional environmental agencies are potentially good sources of information, but their data on industrial emissions and compliance are generally not in the public domain. The World Bank has therefore developed a collaborative program with several environmental agencies to address the need for better information. For the partner agencies, the program provides information on international experience with pollution control, and technical assistance on designing new regulatory programs and evaluating program results. For the World Bank research team, the partner agencies have provided access to information on plant-level pollution and regulation. The Bank team has developed collegial relationships with regulatory agencies in several OECD countries as well.

The fruits of collaboration are well illustrated by a cross-country study of industrial water pollution intensity cited in this chapter (Hettige, Mani, and Wheeler, 1998). For that study, the World Bank team acquired information from 12 countries (Figure B5.1):

Brazil: CETESB, the environmental agency for São Paulo State, provided information on organic water pollution from its 1,250-plant database.

Figure B5.1   Data for Comparative Research

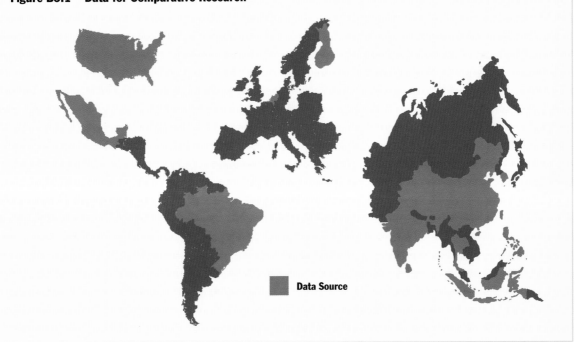

Data Source

111

Box 5.1 *(Continued)*

China: The State Environmental Protection Agency (SEPA) supplied information on water pollution from its comprehensive database on major sources of industrial pollution. Our estimates are based on SEPA's 1993 data for 269 factories scattered throughout China.

Finland: The Industrial Waste Water Office of the National Board of Waters and the Environment provided data on water emissions in 1992 from 193 large water-polluting factories.

India: The Tamil Nadu Pollution Control Board, which monitors air and water pollution for all the manufacturing units in the state, provided plant-level data for 1993–94.

Indonesia: BAPEDAL, Indonesia's National Pollution Control Agency in the Ministry of Environment, provided data on plant-level emissions.

Korea: The National Pollution Control Agency provided 1991 data on water emissions from 13,504 facilities.

Mexico: The State Water Monitoring Authority provided 1994 data on water emissions from 7,500 facilities in the Monterrey Metropolitan Area.

The Netherlands: The Ministry of Housing, Spatial Planning, and the Environment provided 1990 data on water pollution from its

Emissions Inventory System, which encompasses 700 regularly monitored facilities.

Philippines: The Philippine Department of Environment and Natural Resources (DENR) and the Laguna Lake Development Authority provided data on emissions from factories in the Manila area.

Taiwan (China): The Water Quality Protection Division of the Taiwan Environment Protection Agency provided data on emissions from 1,800 plants.

Thailand: Seatec International, a private environmental consulting firm in Bangkok, provided plant-level data on water emissions from 450 facilities in two industrial estates in Rangsit and Suksawat in 1992.

Sri Lanka: The World Bank's Metropolitan Environment Improvement Program and the Sri Lankan Board of Investment supplied data on pollution and employment as part of their study of wastewater treatment options for the Ekala/Ja-ela Industrial Estate. Ekala/Ja-ela, one of two major estates in Sri Lanka, includes 143 industrial establishments with 21,000 employees.

USA: Regional databases provided information on industrial water discharges, collected by the U.S. Environmental Protection Agency.

Source: Hettige, Mani, and Wheeler (1998)

ment costs (MAC) and marginal expected penalties (MEP). The plant's pre-reform pollution intensity is blue (where blue MAC = red MEP). In case 1, when energy prices rise, the cost of abating pollution increases to red, and so does pollution intensity (to the point where red MAC = red MEP). In case 2, with declining subsidies, the plant uses fewer raw materials, waste residuals decline, and the cost of abating pollution falls to green, as does pollution intensity (to the

Figure 5.4 Price Reform and Pollution Intensity

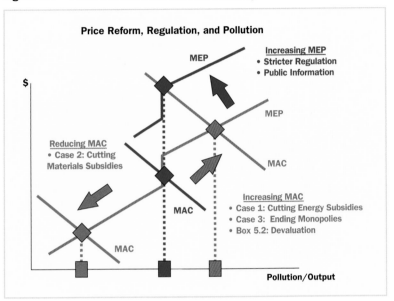

point where green MAC = red MEP). In case 3, the plant's raw materials supplier has lost monopoly power and lowered prices, so the plant uses more materials (generating more waste residuals), MAC increases, and so does pollution intensity.

The value of a country's currency can also affect the prices of chemicals, equipment, and spare parts used for controlling pollution, because developing countries often import such inputs. By making them more expensive, devaluing a country's currency—a common feature of economic reform—should raise pollution intensity by reducing pollution control. The study summarized in Box 5.2 suggests that Indonesia's recent devaluation had this effect.

For clarity, Figure 5.4 assumes that MAC increases by the same amount for reduced energy subsidies, elimination of monopoly power, and devaluation. The plant will return to blue pollution intensity only if MEP is increased from red to blue by stricter formal or informal regulation.

5.3 The Impact of Plant Ownership on Pollution

Economic reforms often change a country's pattern of factory ownership, which in turn affects pollution. The most obvious case is

Box 5.2 Industrial Pollution in Indonesia's Financial Crisis

A recent study analyzed the impact of Indonesia's financial crisis on industrial production and emissions in a large sample of factories (Afsah, 1998). The study confirms that industrial output declined significantly during the crisis—by 18 percent—but also finds that the intensity of factories' organic water pollution rose by 15 percent. The study identifies two main reasons for increased pollution intensity: rapid devaluation of the country's currency, which made imported inputs for curbing pollution much more expensive (raising MAC); and drastic cuts in regulators' budgets (lowering MEP). As plant managers responded to the new conditions, pollution intensity jumped from blue to red (Figure B5.2). However, the country's total emissions of organic water pollutants remained roughly constant, because declining production volume offset the rise in pollution intensity.

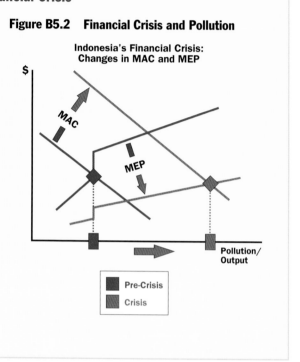

Figure B5.2 Financial Crisis and Pollution

privatization, which transfers state-owned plants to private hands, but trade reform can also decrease the role of family-owned and single-plant firms in the economy while increasing the role of large enterprises (particularly multinationals). State-owned plants worldwide have compiled an unenviable record of wasteful resource use and financial distress, which in turn means higher abatement costs, less investment in pollution control, and higher pollution intensity. Several recent studies have confirmed these effects. A study in Indonesia finds that public enterprises are considerably more pollution intensive than private factories.[10] Analyses in China reveal that state enterprises have higher pollution intensity and lower regulatory compliance than other firms.[11] And a four-country survey of pulp mills in Thailand, Bangladesh, India, and Indonesia shows that state-owned plants make far less effort to abate pollution than their private counterparts.[12]

Although the public enterprises in Indonesia's PROPER program were more compliant than private firms when the program began, after 18 months the record of the two types of enterprises did not differ significantly. We view this as a reflection of the fact—also experienced by CETESB in Cubatao—that state-owned enterprises are less susceptible to outside pressure, so public information exerts less influence on their behavior. If this reasoning is correct, then state-owned enterprises will probably lag behind other firms participating in PROPER in the coming years. Overall, we believe the evidence clearly shows that privatizing state-owned enterprises reduces pollution.

The Uncertain Effect of Family Ownership

In Asia and Latin America, family enterprises have traditionally dominated many industry sectors. In Brazil, for example, two-thirds of the 33 largest private business groups are family controlled, and such groups also dominate in Mexico, Argentina, Colombia, and Chile.[13] Family-controlled firms flourished during the protectionist era because state enforcement of business contracts was uncertain, the absence of international competition reduced pressure to hire professional managers, and limited domestic markets curtailed firms' need for large outside sources of capital. With more open markets and vigorous international trade, the advantages of family-owned business structures have begun to wane.

Like state-owned enterprises, family-owned firms seem likely to be more pollution intensive and less compliant with environmental regulations than publicly traded firms. As we saw in Chapter 3, studies in Mexico and other countries show that the stock market rewards good environmental performance, and a complementary study of Mexican factories shows that plants in publicly traded firms comply with environmental regulations at significantly higher rates than family-owned factories. However, plant-level results from India do not show any compliance differential between family-owned and publicly traded firms. The authors of the India study postulate that better regulatory enforcement in Mexico prompts the Mexican stock market to value environmental performance more highly than the Indian market. However, that interpretation is speculative, and the effect of family ownership on pollution levels remains inconclusive.[14]

The Impact of Multinationals

Conventional wisdom holds that multinationals are greener than domestically owned businesses in developing countries, because multinationals have high-level technical skills, good information about abatement alternatives, internationally competitive management, and better access to capital. Moreover, as "guests" in the local economy, multinationals may be more susceptible to formal and informal pressure from regulators and communities.

However, systematic evidence from studies of plant-level data in Indonesia, Bangladesh, Thailand, India, and Mexico shows that multinationals are not, in fact, greener than publicly traded domestic firms with similar characteristics.[15] Still, the results of Indonesia's PROPER public-disclosure program imply a caveat. Multinationals and private domestic firms were equally compliant with regulations when the program began. However, after 18 months the former complied at significantly higher rates, suggesting that multinationals adjust more rapidly to public information (Box 3.2). Because the Indonesian study does not fully control for ownership status, we do not know whether this effect stems from the fact that a firm is a multinational or that it is publicly traded. The Mexican results cited in Chapter 3 suggest that public trading is the key.

In any case, by overturning the myth of green multinationals, these studies show that environmental progress is a domestic affair. Foreign investment can be valuable for many reasons, but it is unnecessary for effective pollution control.

Consolidating Ownership

As countries open their borders to trade and reduce the state's role in the economy, larger, more sophisticated operations that can withstand competition begin absorbing single-plant firms. As we saw in Chapter 4, these changes can boost environmental performance, because larger firms can spread the costs of in-house technical services over more factories. Plant-level analyses in several countries confirm this advantage. A recent study in Mexico also found that multiplant status improves regulatory compliance. (We might expect multiplant firms to attract more attention from regulators, but a recent study in India found that multiplant status has no effect on the rate at which regulators inspect a company.)[16]

Reduced state intervention in the economy generally translates into larger factories in pollution-intensive industries, although this is not inevitable. The Soviet Union constructed huge steel plants with scant regard for the cost of transporting raw materials and steel, and in the post-Soviet era downsizing has reigned as transportation costs have risen. State enterprises in other economies have faced similar problems. However, economic reforms usually increase plant size. Recent work in the Philippines has suggested that larger manufacturing plants are more economically efficient.[17] As Box 5.3 shows, market reform in China has led to a major consolidation of production. In India, many small plants survive only because they are protected by law.

Figure 5.5 draws on four econometric studies to depict the country-wide results of consolidation: Merging two smaller hypothetical plants whose production and pollution levels originally total 100 units would cut overall pollution to about 70 units in Mexico and India and 80 units in China and Indonesia.[18]

However, even though it reduces pollution intensity, consolidation may inflict more overall pollution damage because large plants tend to cluster in populous areas. For example, a recent study in Brazil stratified 3,500 municipalities into 10 groups by income per capita and examined the location of 156,000 factories of various sizes. Figure 5.6 shows that large plants locate in wealthier regions, which also tend to have the largest populations (Box 2.2). Even though the large plants are less pollution intensive, more people die from air pollution because more of them live close to the plants.[19]

Thus, unless regulators tighten pollution control, the net effect of consolidation may be more pollution damage. Fortunately, large plants are also natural targets for regulators with limited monitoring and enforcement capability. Strategies that focus on major polluters, such as CETESB's ABC approach, can lower pollution intensity to compensate for greater population exposure. Even where regulation is weak, local communities can more easily identify large plants and pressure them to reduce pollution.

5.4 Accounting for Pollution's Hidden Half

Overall, economic reform reduces pollution intensity by cutting subsidies for raw materials and encouraging international trade, privatization of state enterprises, more publicly traded firms, and larger firms and plants. However, economic reforms do not always reduce pollution: Accelerated output growth may overwhelm cuts in pollution intensity. And devaluing a country's currency, removing energy subsidies, and eliminating monopolies on production of raw materials may actually increase pollution intensity in some cases. Furthermore, consolidation may bring more large plants to urban areas, increasing the impact of pollution on human health.

The bottom line is that environmentalists can welcome most reforms as pollution fighters, but economic reformers should recognize that their efforts can produce perverse environmental impacts.

Box 5.3 Economic Reform and Industrial Pollution in China

To determine the impact of China's economic reform on industrial pollution, we developed comparative statistics for five provinces in central and eastern China (Figure B5.3a). Four of these provinces (including the Beijing and Shanghai metropolitan regions) are scattered from north to south in China's eastern coastal region. Beijing's industry has a diversity that reflects its status as the nation's political capital. Liaoning is a traditional center of heavy industry, and many of its factories rely on old, highly polluting processes. Shanghai's industrial base

Figure B5.3a   Chinese Provinces

Five Industrial Regions in Central and Eastern China

is extremely diverse but its sheer scale assures a large potential pollution problem. Guangdong's development has brought rapid growth of light manufacturing. Finally, Sichuan, located in the Red Basin in south-central China, is considerably poorer than the other four provinces, and its industry is highly pollution intensive.

China's economic reforms have significantly changed average plant size and ownership patterns in these five provinces. The econ-

Figure B5.3b   Plant Size and Ownership

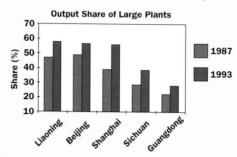

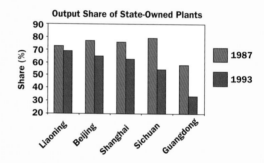

omy's share of large plants consistently grew from 1987 to 1993, most markedly in Shanghai, while the share of state-owned enterprises (SOEs) declined, particularly in Sichuan and Guangdong (Figure B5.3b).

The econometric results reported in Dasgupta, Wang, and Wheeler (1997) suggest that both larger plants and a smaller role for SOEs should reduce industry's pollution intensity. Figure B5.3c illustrates this result for organic water pollution (chemical oxygen demand (COD)) and air pollution (TSP). At the provincial level, emissions intensities for both types of pollution have declined significantly during the period of economic reform. The greatest absolute declines have occurred in Sichuan

Box 5.3 *(Continued)*

Figure B5.3c   Pollution Intensities and Reform

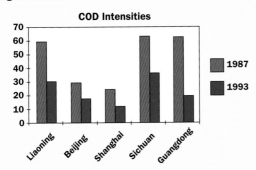

Figure B5.3d   Dirty Sectors in China

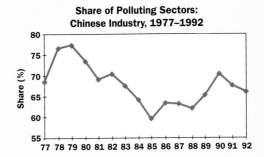

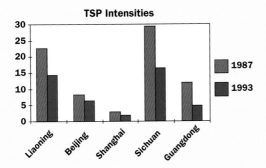

and Guangdong, but all five provinces have seen pollution intensities drop.

Concern about possible "pollution havens" in east Asia might focus on China, because the country has weaker environmental regulations and lower prices for heavy raw materials than many of its trading partners. To see whether polluting industries have flourished under these conditions, we analyzed recent trends for the five dirtiest sectors: chemicals, pulp and paper, nonferrous metals, ferrous metals, and nonmetallic minerals (principally cement).* We found that the national output share of these five highly polluting sectors actually declined during the reform period (Figure B5.3d). Thus, for China, opening the economy to more trade has not produced a shift toward dirty industries.

* For identification of polluting sectors, see Mani and Wheeler (1998) and Hettige, Martin, Singh, and Wheeler (1994).

Careful analysis of such effects by both economists and environmentalists—as well as collaboration between them—is essential. Fortunately, as we will show in Chapter 6, sophisticated use of information technology can help regulators focus on the worst polluters and enlist communities in keeping them in line. To sustain such efforts and ensure their success, policymakers will have to devote some of the dividends from economic reform to improving environmental information and regulation.

Figure 5.5   Plant Size and Pollution

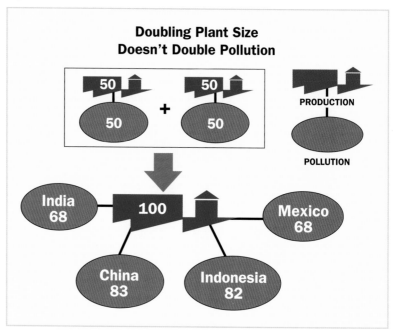

Source: See End Note 16

Figure 5.6   Plant Size and Regional Development

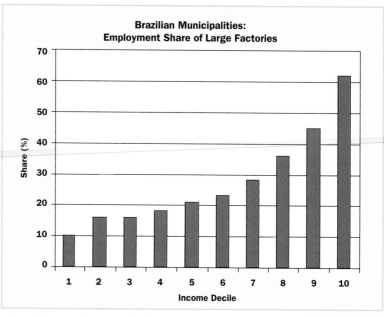

Source: Dasgupta, Lucas, and Wheeler (1998)

References

Afsah, S., 1998, "Impact of Financial Crisis on Industrial Growth and Environmental Performance in Indonesia," (Washington: US-Asia Environmental Partnership), July.

CETESB, 1986, "Restoring the Serra do Mar."

———, 1990, "Cubatao: A Change of Air."

———, 1994, "Acao da CETESB em Cubatao: Situacao em Junho de 1994."

Birdsall, N., and D. Wheeler, 1993, "Trade Policy and Industrial Pollution in Latin America: Where Are The Pollution Havens?" *Journal of Environment and Development*, Vol. 2, No. 1, Winter.

Dasgupta, S., H. Hettige, and D. Wheeler, 1997, "What Improves Environmental Performance? Evidence from Mexican Industry," World Bank Development Research Group Working Paper, No. 1877, December.

Dasgupta, S., M. Huq, and D. Wheeler, 1997, "Bending the Rules: Discretionary Pollution Control in China," World Bank Development Research Group Working Paper, No. 1761, February.

Dasgupta, S., R. Lucas, and D. Wheeler, 1997, "Small Plants, Pollution and Poverty: Evidence from Mexico and Brazil," World Bank Development Research Group Working Paper, No. 2029, November.

Dasgupta, S., H. Wang, and D. Wheeler, 1997, "Surviving Success: Policy Reform and the Future of Industrial Pollution in China," World Bank Policy Research Department Working Paper, No. 1856, October.

Dollar, D., 1992, "Outward-Oriented Developing Economies Really Do Grow More Rapidly: Evidence from 95 LDCs, 1976–1985," *Economic Development and Cultural Change*, 523–44.

Economist, The, 1997a, "A Very Big Deal," Dec. 6.

———, 1997b, "Inside Story," Dec. 6.

Hartman, R., M. Huq, and D. Wheeler, 1997, "Why Paper Mills Clean Up: Determinants of Pollution Abatement in Four Asian Countries," World Bank Policy Research Department Working Paper, No. 1710, January.

Hettige, H., R. Lucas, and D. Wheeler, 1992, "The Toxic Intensity of Industrial Production: Global Patterns, Trends, and Trade Policy," *American Economic Review Papers and Proceedings*, May.

Hettige, H., M. Mani, and D. Wheeler, 1998, "Industrial Pollution in Economic Development: Kuznets Revisited," World Bank Development Research Group Working Paper, No. 1876, January.

Hettige, H., P. Martin, M. Singh, and D.Wheeler, 1994, "The Industrial Pollution Projection System," World Bank Policy Research Department Working Paper, No. 1431, December.

Mani, M., and D. Wheeler, 1998, "In Search of Pollution Havens? Dirty Industry in the World Economy, 1960–1995," *Journal of Environment and Development*, September.

Mini, F., and E. Rodriguez, 1998, "Are SMEs More Efficient? Revisiting Efficiency Indicators in a Philippine Manufacturing Sector," World Bank, Operations Evaluation Department.

Pargal, S., M. Huq, and M. Mani, 1997, "Inspections and Emissions in India: Puzzling Survey Evidence on Industrial Water Pollution," World Bank Development Research Group Working Paper, No. 1810, August.

Pargal, S., and D. Wheeler, 1996, "Informal Regulation of Industrial Pollution in Developing Countries: Evidence From Indonesia," *Journal of Political Economy*, Vol. 104, No. 6, 1314 + .

Wang, H., and D. Wheeler, 1996, "Pricing Industrial Pollution In China: An Econometric Analysis of the Levy System," World Bank Policy Research Department Working Paper, No. 1644, September.

——, 1999, "China's Pollution Levy: An Analysis of Industry's Response," presented to the Association of Environmental and Resource Economists (AERE) Workshop, "Market-Based Instruments for Environmental Protection," John F. Kennedy School of Government, Harvard University, July 18–20.

Wheeler, D., M. Huq, and P. Martin, 1993, "Process Change, Economic Policy, and Industrial Pollution: Cross Country Evidence from the Wood Pulp and Steel Industries," presented at the Annual Meeting, American Economic Association, Anaheim, California, January.

End Notes

1. Sources for the Cubatao story include CETESB (1986, 1990, 1994) and several visits to the area by the authors. CETESB stands for Companhia de Technologia de Saneamento Ambiental.

2. For a description of CETESB's ABC targeting strategy, see Chapter 2.

3. See *The Economist* (1997a). COSIPA stands for Companhia Siderúrgica Paulista.

4. Wheeler, Huq, and Martin (1993).

5. See Wheeler, Huq, and Martin (1993). We identified open and closed economies using a measure developed by Dollar (1992).

6. See Birdsall and Wheeler (1993), and Hettige, Lucas, and Wheeler (1992).

7. See Box 3.2, Pargal, Huq, and Mani (1998), and Dasgupta, Hettige, and Wheeler (1997).

8. For econometric evidence on materials prices and plant-level pollution intensity, see Pargal and Wheeler (1996).

9. These research projects included a 12-country study at the World Bank (Box 5.1) and country studies for India and Indonesia. See Hettige, Mani, and Wheeler (1998), Pargal, Huq, and Mani (1997), and Pargal and Wheeler (1996).

10. See Pargal and Wheeler (1996).

11. See Wang and Wheeler (1996) and Dasgupta, Huq, and Wheeler (1997).

12. See Hartman, Huq, and Wheeler (1997).

13. See *The Economist* (1997b).

14. See Dasgupta, Hettige, and Wheeler (1997), and Pargal, Huq, and Mani (1997).

15. References: India and Thailand: Hartman, Huq, and Wheeler (1997); Indonesia: Pargal and Wheeler (1996); Mexico: Dasgupta, Hettige, and Wheeler (1997).

16. References: India: Pargal, Huq, and Mani (1997); China: Wang and Wheeler (1999); Indonesia: Pargal and Wheeler (1996); Mexico: Dasgupta, Hettige, and Wheeler (1997).

17. See Mini and Rodriguez (1998).

18. See End Note 16.

19. See Dasgupta, Lucas, and Wheeler (1998).

Sepetiba

Guanabara

1970

1990

Algae ★★
- ● 1 - 5
- ○ 5 - 10
- ○ 10 - 15
- ● 15 - 32

* Chlorophyll (ug / l)

Total Coliforms*
- ● 0 - 100
- ○ 100 - 500
- ○ 1000 - 2000
- ● 2000 - 25000

* MPN / 100ml

The Bays of Rio: FEEMA's Challenge

Source: Nélio Ricardo Aguiar, 3WayNet Assessoria de Propaganda e Marketing; Nilo Lima Fotografo

Map provided by www.mapquest.com

Chapter Six

Managing
and Sustaining Reform

From the top of Corcovado Mountain, Rio de Janeiro is a breath-taking study in contradictions. The view sweeps from Ipanema's luxury apartments and golden beaches in the south to the storied entrance to Guanabara Bay in the east. Yet the scene also includes the mountainside shanties of the Favela Roçinha and the industrial suburb of São Cristóvão, both part of the "other" Rio—the crowded, polluted, poor communities that are home to most of the city's people.

The top floor of the tallest building in São Cristóvão houses FEEMA, Rio State's environmental protection agency. On many mornings, FEEMA's staff cannot even see nearby Guanabara Bay because the smog is too dense. Nor would a close-up view of the bay provide a pleasing spectacle in any case, as its inshore waters are brown and effectively dead, starved of oxygen by organic pollution from sewage and industrial waste. Once a showcase for Rio's beauty, Guanabara now languishes as a dirty backwater. South of the city, Sepetiba Bay appears to be headed in the same direction.

Rio's air and water pollution seriously threaten its intended future as a center for world business and tourism, and its environmental decline has saddled the region's people with increased illness, the loss of once-thriving fisheries, and fewer recreational opportunities. Rio's environment has deteriorated for many reasons, but FEEMA's declining effectiveness ranks high on the list.[1] In the 1980s, the agency suffered from a loss of political support, reduced budgets, and an obsolete administrative system.

One afternoon in 1996, an impromptu street celebration marked the beginning of a new era for the agency. Employees applauded as a truck pulled away, carrying the archaic minicomputer that had housed the agency's central records. Served by a small priesthood of technicians who generated occasional reports, the machine had been effectively off-limits to the departments charged with environmental planning, factory inspections, and enforcement. Most records had been shelved in moldering folders or desultorily entered into a stand-alone PC that remained the exclusive province of a departmental manager. So the agency had operated for a decade, with minimal co-ordination and internal communication.

As the minicomputer-laden truck departed, a new networked PC system began operating upstairs, symbolizing a fundamental change in the agency's approach. The network allowed departments to store their records in a common database that any unit could tap. The system reflected the agency's fresh approach to regulation: FEEMA's new president insisted on moving beyond legalistic, end-of-pipe regulation to strategies that reflected assessments of overall benefits and costs for Rio State.

Responding to the new mandate, agency managers began asking for reports that combined information from different departments. The effectiveness of the agency's technical staff increased as the networked database enabled them to analyze emissions trends, community complaints, inspection reports, and readings from air and water monitoring stations, such as those in Guanabara and Sepetiba Bays. The agency's new geographic information system made a contribution by instantly combining maps of water quality, air quality, population centers, and pollution sources, allowing staff members to identify the worst environmental problems and polluters.

Of course, FEEMA's renewal stemmed from far more than the technical fix offered by networked PCs. Like their counterparts in Ciudad Juárez, Mexico, FEEMA's leaders emphasized community participation in planning and implementing regulations—which in turn required public education on environmental quality, goals, progress, and the regulatory status of major sources of pollution. With its new system, FEEMA was well positioned to supply this information in compelling, graphical formats. To capitalize on public involvement, the agency began considering a polluter rating system like Indonesia's PROPER program.

FEEMA also focused on a more productive relationship with the business community. The agency had traditionally regulated through continuous low-level negotiations with factory managers. In the new approach, FEEMA's president met with industry leaders to develop a consensus on environmental objectives for the state. Progressive CEOs supported this approach, because they envisioned Rio as an environmentally friendly headquarters city for international business. FEEMA's managers also negotiated commitments from industry groups that entailed collective responsibility for failure to meet pollution control objectives. Since the agency was better equipped to provide information on the condition of the environment and priorities for action, the business community listened to its proposals with enhanced respect.

FEEMA's third outreach effort focused on developing closer relationships with the World Bank and other international agencies. Like FEEMA, those institutions had begun shifting from a focus on end-of-pipe regulation to promotion of flexible regulatory instruments, government-industry cooperation, and the use of benefit-cost analysis to determine priorities. The Bank and other institutions provided financial and technical support for the agency's new information system, helped develop action plans, and sponsored specific projects for reducing air and water pollution in Rio de Janeiro State.

Environmental reform in Rio resembles many other renewal initiatives, in which regulators are using decentralized information technology to assess their options and develop cost-effective programs based on multiple sources of data. New technology has cut the cost of gathering, processing, and distributing this information, enabling regulators to mediate environmental agreements between communities and businesses more effectively. More cooperative relationships have, in turn, encouraged stronger political support for environmental policy reforms.[2]

6.1 The Contribution of Information Systems

Timely, accurate, and well-packaged information is critical to the new approach. To illustrate an effective environmental information system, consider a hypothetical case of river pollution. Emissions from diverse activities along the river—a large factory, numerous small ones, a farming district, and a riverside community—cause water to decline in quality as it moves downstream.

Because staff skills and time are limited, the local environmental agency focuses on accurately tracking critical water pollutants rather than maintaining an unwieldy catalog of all possible emissions data.

The agency's priorities include heavy metals, fecal coliforms, biological oxygen demand (BOD), and phosphorus (Figure 6.1): The first two pollutants pose serious threats to human health, while the latter two damage ecosystems.

The agency requires all plants along the river to submit periodic reports, certified by outside auditors, on emissions of these substances. The reports are usually accurate because the agency blacklists dishonest auditors, putting them out of business. The agency uses random, surprise inspections to keep the probability of discovering false reports high.

Monitoring devices in the river further confirm the reported emissions and measure their impact. This effort feeds standard, user-friendly database software and relies on a dispersion model, built by the agency's technical team, that tracks pollution using data on the river's flow rate, volume, temperature, and other factors.

The first upstream monitor in Figure 6.1 records no significant pollution (all ratings are blue). Regulators know that a large food-processing plant downstream dumps a heavy BOD load into the river, and farther downstream a complex of small tanneries and textile mills reports substantial emissions of heavy metals and additional BOD. A second river monitor shows that these discharges significantly affect water quality, and the information system rates BOD or-

Figure 6.1   Monitoring Pollution

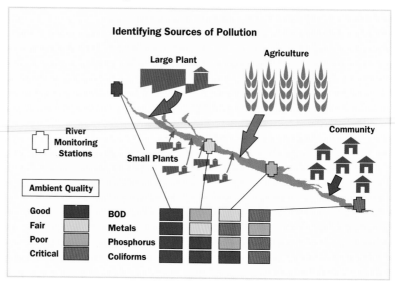

ange and metals yellow. Below the industrial area several large farms abut the river; a third monitor reveals a heavy phosphorus load from fertilizer runoff, and the system rates that element orange. The monitor also indicates that the river has assimilated some BOD, so its rating improves to yellow, while the rating for metals becomes red.

Finally, the river flows past a community that discharges untreated sewage laden with BOD, fecal coliforms, and phosphorus from household detergents. The fourth monitoring station rates BOD and coliforms red, although metals improve to orange because some have settled to the bottom, later to appear in the tissues of fish. The rating for phosphorus becomes red from the combination of agricultural runoff and community wastewater.

As the river leaves the monitored area, it is for all practical purposes dead. Contaminated by pathogens, its water is dangerous to drink or swim in, its dissolved oxygen level is too low to support many species of fish, the metals content is too high for people to safely consume any fish that remain, and algae affect the water's color and odor. Communities farther downstream will bear heavy costs from this pollution.

The agency has now met its first three responsibilities: identifying major pollution sources, monitoring their effluent, and analyzing the effect on environmental quality. The computer system links to a geographic information system that enables users to call up tables and maps that report ambient quality at each point on the river, along with information about polluters' characteristics, emissions and compliance status (Figure 6.2).

Choosing a Plan of Action

Although data on pollution sources and ambient quality provide critical information, policymakers must further analyze the results to determine their most cost-effective response. Toward that end, the agency's technical team uses the database and the best available models to estimate pollution-related damage to human health and losses of aquatic life, recreational amenities, and economic output. The team also uses the characteristics of polluters to identify those that can respond rapidly and at low cost to tighter regulation (Figure 6.3).

Taking these factors into account, policymakers then develop a strategy that identifies the pollutants to be regulated, ambient quality goals, a timetable for reaching them, and appropriate regulatory instruments: pollution charges, tradable permits, or emissions stan-

Figure 6.2   Data Collection

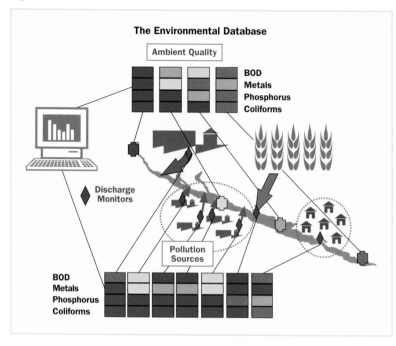

dards. The regulators must also decide which sources to target, taking note of factories' importance as local employers and other politically sensitive issues. In practice, the regulators know that their effectiveness depends on constant feedback and long-term support from all the groups affected by regulation.

6.2 Creating Coalitions for Change

Credibility is the irreplaceable currency of regulation, as regulators' political influence and budgetary support will plummet if the public believes that an agency is corrupt or incompetent. Polluters will also resist regulation more easily if credibility falls, and the news media will discount information provided by the agency.

Environmental reformers have discovered three keys to maintaining the precious asset of credibility: focus, transparency, and community participation. For resource-strapped agencies in developing countries, focus provides the best protection against operational failure and loss of reputation. Agencies can avoid serious trouble if they target a small group of serious polluters, limit regulation to a few critical pollutants, effectively measure these pollutants as well

Figure 6.3   Analysis

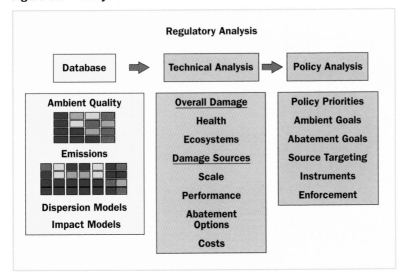

as regulatory compliance, and publicly document their activities. Agencies whose ambitions outrun their resources may look good for awhile, but their credibility will fade as factual errors and misjudgments accumulate on the public record.

Transparency provides the second key to credibility because it prevents corruption. Corruption at higher levels of management can fester for a long time without detection, and even if managers are honest, secrecy may tempt individual inspectors to take payoffs that may dwarf their salaries. Without public information, communities have no way of knowing whether regulators are doing their job. The solution to the secrecy problem is clear: consistent, unbiased disclosure of polluters' emissions, local environmental impacts, inspection results, and enforcement actions. Chapter 3 has discussed innovative disclosure programs in several Asian and Latin American countries; Box 6.1 describes the process that ensures credibility for Indonesia's PROPER rating system.

Earlier policy experiments in Brazil illustrate the importance of information integrity in pollution disclosure programs. During the late 1970s, the pollution control agencies of Rio and São Paulo States attempted to pressure the most serious polluters by announcing their names to the media. Both agencies were sued by the firms whose names were published. In São Paulo, CETESB's program survived the court challenge because it could provide solid evidence to

Box 6.1 PROPER: Building Credibility

Indonesia's public rating system for polluters has significantly reduced emissions and attracted strong popular support. Still, the program was delayed a year, until mid-1995, because BAPEDAL's leaders realized that it would succeed only if the public understood the ratings, trusted the underlying information, and believed in the honesty of PROPER's managers.

The ratings strategy relied on public communication. By summarizing complex information in a single five-color rating scheme, PROPER allowed the public to compare polluters across many locations and industry sectors. The ratings also made it easy for the media to show which factories complied with regulations and which did not.

Data integrity presented a significant challenge. The agency had relatively little experience with collecting, verifying, and analyzing large amounts of information, so PROPER had some false starts before the Minister of the Environment was satisfied with the rating system. Finally, with the assistance of technical teams from the World Bank, Canada, Australia and the United States, BAPEDAL developed a reliable system for monitoring, recording, and analyzing water emissions from a pilot sample of factories.

To enhance credibility with all stakeholders, BAPEDAL developed a careful process for

Figure B6.1 Steps in Developing PROPER

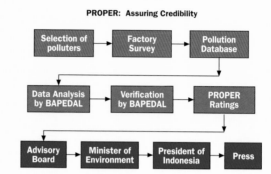

Source: Shakeb Afsah; BAPEDAL

vetting the ratings through three checkpoints: an advisory board, with representatives from academia, industry, other government agencies and environmental NGOs; the Environment Minister; and finally the President himself (Figure B6.1). The first ratings emerged from these checks unscathed, and their effect on the business community was compounded by the knowledge that the President of Indonesia had approved them.

These careful measures have paid off. PROPER has maintained its reputation for consistency and objectivity, and the public has continued to support it despite Indonesia's political and financial crisis.

support its claims. After the court rejected the lawsuit, most blacklisted firms quickly reduced pollution enough to remove themselves from the spotlight. In Rio, by contrast, FEEMA's data were too weak to withstand the court challenge. The lawsuit succeeded, and the Rio disclosure program collapsed.[3]

Widespread participation also builds public credibility. Politics and the theater share an important trait: Once actors have appeared onstage, their existence becomes part of the drama. The audience assigns them a role that cannot be vacated without comment or justification. Successful environmental reformers exploit this principle by crowding the public stage with leaders from communities that confront major pollution problems. Once these leaders come on-stage, political opponents of environmental reform can no longer ignore them, and their presence helps insure that the agency itself will not be co-opted by special interests. Despite the importance of expanded community participation, however, not all regulators may welcome it. Power is seldom ceded willingly, and reformers' most difficult task may be persuading some of their own colleagues to support participatory approaches.

An effective regulatory system promotes two-way communication with participants. As communities and markets gain access to environmental information, pressure through many new channels can prompt polluters to reduce their emissions (Figure 6.4). Feedback from the public is also critical: Effective regulators must understand and act upon communities' environmental concerns. Toward this end, Mexico's Environment Ministry is establishing community centers that automatically log, categorize, and route citizens' complaints about pollution to the appropriate authorities. Such systems allow regulators to identify areas with serious problems, and also enable citizens to monitor responses to their complaints.

6.3 The Politics of Sustaining Reform

Environmental reforms are often difficult to sustain. As governments change, high-level sympathy for environmental regulation

Figure 6.4 Reactions to Public Information

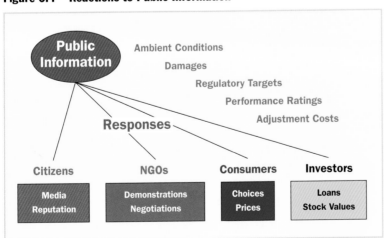

may wax and wane. Even if they support existing programs, politically appointed environment ministers seldom enter office with deep knowledge of pollution problems. To remain effective, agency staff members must continually sell their programs, developing political skills and long-term budgetary strategies along with technical competence.

Securing the Budget

Traditional public-finance theory acknowledges that pollution charges and fines provide useful incentives to reduce emissions, but it also holds that regulators should remit revenues to the regional or national government. By drawing on all tax and penalty revenues, the government can fund social, educational, or environmental programs with the highest benefit-cost ratios.

If the government had perfect foresight, Platonic neutrality, and seamless administrative efficiency, no one could quarrel with this approach. Spending would encompass not only current programs but also long-term investment, and public planners would assure stability in the flow of funds. Unfortunately, many regulators, especially those in developing countries, do not inhabit such a world: The political process is quirky, unstable, and prone to sudden crises that drain available budgets.

Regulators also face continual challenges from threatened interests. While some industrialists have strategic vision and support effective regulation, others remain fixated on the short-run bottom line. The most recalcitrant will lobby their political allies for cutbacks in regulators' budgets, and may be joined by some labor leaders who view stricter pollution control as a threat to jobs.

Confronted daily by these realities, regulators often attempt to retain control over pollution charges and fines because they are secure funding sources. Retaining some control also gives regulators stronger incentives to collect fines from polluters. Agencies' desire to keep revenues out of central hands sits well with local politicians and business leaders, who want to see local payments used to support local environmental programs. Environmental reformers must often heed these views because hostile businesses and politicians can block new programs.

Colombia's pollution charge program moved forward when regulators, industrialists, and public sewerage authorities agreed to use part of the revenues to support the regional regulatory agencies, and to invest the rest in local environmental projects (Box 6.2). Although traditional public-finance theory does not support such an approach,

Box 6.2 Sharing the Funds in Colombia

Chapter 2 described Colombia's new regulatory system, which charges polluters for each unit of emissions. Under the standards-based system, regional environmental agencies had legal authority to fine plants that failed to comply with regulations. Reality often dictated otherwise, however, because enforcement procedures were cumbersome and susceptible to legal delaying tactics. The new pollution charge system jettisons criminal sanctions: Plants are free to pollute and pay, but the charges are high enough to affect managers' cost calculations significantly.

When the program first took shape in Colombia's Environment Ministry, the design team focused on technical issues, working to estimate abatement costs and set charges that would reduce pollution significantly without bankrupting polluters. However, once the team moved to the field, it quickly found that political issues eclipsed technical ones. Polluters themselves defined a central concern: Once they paid, who would get the money? The regional agencies laid claim to some of the funds, because they wanted financial insulation from the political funding cycle. Local business and public works managers accepted that idea but refused to countenance remitting the balance to the national treasury. They weren't impressed by the argument that charges would automatically improve the environment by encouraging cost-minimizing plants to reduce pollution. Instead, they viewed the charges as a financial sacrifice they would bear only if the revenues were used to fund local investments in cleaner manufacturing and wastewater treatment.

Without support from industrialists and public works managers, the charge program stood no chance of implementation. Tough negotiations loomed, and the regional environmental agencies enlisted community-based or-

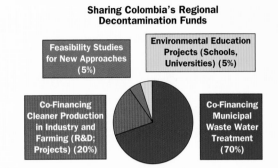

Figure B6.2   Using Pollution Charge Revenues

Sharing Colombia's Regional Decontamination Funds

- Feasibility Studies for New Approaches (5%)
- Environmental Education Projects (Schools, Universities) (5%)
- Co-Financing Cleaner Production in Industry and Farming (R&D; Projects) (20%)
- Co-Financing Municipal Waste Water Treatment (70%)

Source: Colombian Environment Ministry

ganizations as allies on their side of the table. Finally, representatives from the Environment Ministry team, regional agencies, industrialists, public works managers, and community organizations hammered out a mutually agreeable solution. The new charge program would support "regional decontamination funds" used for local environmental projects, after some portion was diverted to fund agency budgets. Figure B6.2 summarizes the Environment Ministry's recommendations for use of the funds, which most regional authorities have followed.

Public finance theory does not countenance the diversion of charge revenues to purely environmental projects, but in reality the program designers had no choice: no regional funds, no program. The ministry team accepted the package and, in an ingenious twist, enlisted one of Colombia's top commercial banks to collect the pollution charges (for a percentage fee), administer the funds to get maximum interest, and disburse them to approved projects. That solution unburdened the local agencies, which had little expertise in billing, collecting, and disbursing, while it encouraged private-sector polluters to pay in order to preserve their credit ratings.

the program's strengths have clearly outweighed this conceptual "flaw." Pollution charges represent a leap forward in regulatory efficiency for Colombia, and the local funding mechanism ensures some measure of long-term stability and effectiveness.

However, accepting political reality does not imply uncritical acceptance of any funding scheme. The designers of Colombia's system have stressed the application of clear benefit-cost criteria to local financing of pollution reduction projects. Useful projects may include public wastewater treatment facilities and support for improved environmental management in small and medium enterprises (Chapter 4). Subsidized loans to private firms for end-of-pipe abatement are probably ill-advised in most cases. Numerous international studies have shown that large firms often gain access to the funds simply because their staffs can produce good technical proposals. Yet such firms will generally clean up anyway, if pollution charges or other instruments provide the right incentives.[4]

Success Stories

Three countries where regulators have adopted new programs illustrate the political aspects of successful reform.[5]

The Colombian pollution charge program has developed strong coalitions of stakeholders in many of its administrative regions. As described in Chapter 2, regulators in each region mediate negotiations between industries and communities on pollution reduction targets and schedules for raising charges if the targets are not met. This participatory approach has created strong community support for the program and has helped insulate it from its political and bureaucratic opponents.

To reinforce community support, the program's promoters are also pushing for a complementary public disclosure program like Indonesia's PROPER. They view it as a powerful vehicle for environmental education as well as a means of addressing public distrust of governmental institutions. The program's promoters also believe that more-precise knowledge of local pollution sources will mobilize communities to confront polluters informally, as well as negotiate with them formally over pollution targets and charges.

In Indonesia, where developers of PROPER also relied on community support, some environmental NGOs initially feared that the program's use of the media would co-opt their traditional role as community advocates. To ensure NGO support, BAPEDAL, Indonesia's environmental agency, invited NGO leaders to join the advisory group that reviewed industry ratings before they were publicly announced. The NGOs accepted, principally because they had a long-standing relationship with BAPEDAL's Deputy for Pollution Control.

BAPEDAL also enlisted support for PROPER from progressive business leaders. Program designers were well aware that large, technically sophisticated companies like PT Indah Kiat could earn good ratings from PROPER (Chapter 3), and they expected CEOs of such firms to support the program as a source of competitive advantage. But the PROPER team also went out of its way to avoid antagonizing firms whose ratings were initially subpar, by precisely identifying the reasons for the poor ratings, suggesting actions to improve them, and offering a grace period before formally announcing the ratings. Agency officials also met regularly with company managers to address their concerns. To further ensure long-term support, an endorsement from Indonesia's President accompanied PROPER's initial ratings, and the Vice President publicly announced the highest-rated factories as part of Indonesia's Earth Day activities.

The developers of Philippines' EcoWatch disclosure program pursued a similar political strategy. The nation's President formally announced EcoWatch along with leaders of the Philippines Business Association, who encouraged association members to participate in the program. The President reiterated his support in speeches and public announcements, and the program allowed poorly rated factories a grace period before public disclosure.

6.4 Living with Change

Politics remains the art of the possible, and no reform of environmental policy can anticipate all untoward events. Political turmoil is a fact of life in many developing countries, and sudden crises or larger political forces can undermine even successful programs with solid support. In Ciudad Juárez, a decision by the Mexican Government to end subsidies for propane undermined a successful program to induce small-scale brick makers to switch to cleaner fuels. Indonesia's financial crisis has made imported pollution-control inputs more expensive and forced cuts in regulators' budgets, reversing some of the gains made under PROPER.

Nevertheless, many well-packaged reforms have proven remarkably durable in the face of rapid political change, including all three programs discussed in this chapter (Box 6.3). We credit much of this survival to the political entrepreneurship of the programs' designers, and to their respect for three fundamental principles of innovative regulation: focus, transparency, and community participation.

Box 6.3 Sustaining Reforms in the Face of Political Change

Environmental policy reforms remain vulnerable to political change until they are fully institutionalized. Figure B6.3 illustrates how expanding elections in developing countries have increased the pace of political change. Nevertheless, as the following examples show, strong programs with wide popular appeal have repeatedly survived turnover in national governments.

Colombia

In 1993, Colombia's Congress established the Ministry of Environment and the "polluter pays" concept as a fundamental principle of Colombian law. In 1997 the Ministry's Office of

Economic Analysis translated this principle into policy by establishing a nationwide pollution charge program. Implementation began when CORNARE, a regional agency near Medellín, started billing local factories for emissions in 1998.

The program has since operated under three different environment ministers: Jose Vicente Mogollon (1996–1997), Eduardo Verano de la Rosa (1997–1998), and Juan Mayr Maldonado (1998–present). The latter took office when Andres Pastrana Arango of the Conservative Party defeated Horacio Serpa of the Liberal Party to win the presidency. Although the

Figure B6.3   Elections in Developing Countries

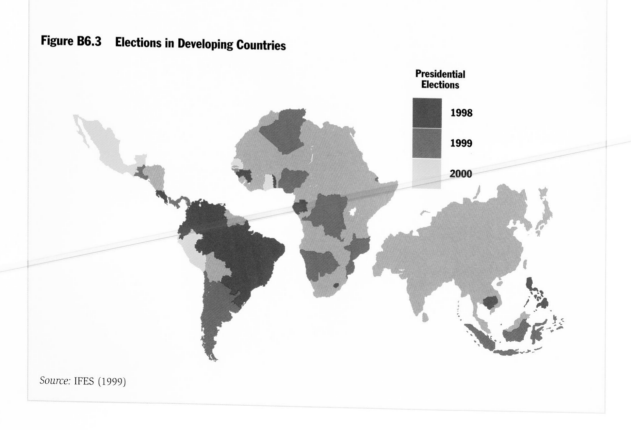

Source: IFES (1999)

Box 6.3 *(Continued)*

national administration has changed, support for pollution charges continues because the program's local constituencies remain politically potent.

Indonesia

In 1993, BAPEDAL's Deputy for Pollution Control proposed PROPER to Indonesia's Environment Minister, Sarwono Kusumaatmadja. After careful development, the program moved to pilot implementation in mid-1995, and was considered a major policy success of the Suharto government. Then in mid-1997, Indonesia's financial and political crisis hit. During the ensuing turbulence PROPER has operated under two new environment ministers: Wijoyo Sudarsono and Sergir Panangian. The BAPEDAL Deputy who developed PROPER has left the agency, and it has endured budget cuts along with other environmental programs. Nevertheless, popular support for the program remains strong and it continues to operate. Original plans to rate 2,000 factories by the year 2000 now look ambitious, but the program expects to have ratings for some 500 factories by the end of 1999.

Philippines

Many countries watched the development of PROPER, but none more closely than the neighboring Philippines. In 1996, Secretary Victor Ramos of the Department of Environment and Natural Resources (DENR) launched a similar program, called EcoWatch. President Fidel Ramos publicly supported the program, which began by focusing on organic water pollution in the national capital region. Within 18 months EcoWatch coverage expanded from 52 to 83 major polluters, and their regulatory compliance rate jumped from 8 percent to 58 percent. This successful introduction attracted widespread support from the media, community leaders, and environmental NGOs.

After the 1998 elections, DENR Secretary Ramos left office along with President Ramos, and President-elect Jose Ejercito Estrada appointed Antonio Cerilles as the new Secretary of DENR. After taking stock, the new administration decided to continue EcoWatch because many of its constituents supported the program. DENR now plans a rapid expansion of EcoWatch to cover major polluters throughout the country.

References

Hanrahan, D., M. Keene, D. Shaman, and D. Wheeler, 1998, "Developing Partnerships for Effective Pollution Management," *Environment Matters at the World Bank*, Annual Review.

IFES (International Foundation for Election Systems), 1999, "IFES Elections Calendar," available at *http://www.ifes.org/eleccal.htm.*

Lovei, M., 1995, "Financing Pollution Abatement: Theory and Practice," World Bank Environment Department Paper, No. 28.

Von Amsberg, J., 1996, Brazil: Managing Environmental Pollution in the State of Rio de Janeiro, World Bank, Brazil Department, Report No. 15488-BR, August.

———, 1997, Brazil: Managing Pollution Problems, The Brown Environmental Agenda, World Bank, Brazil Department, Report No. 16635-BR, June.

World Bank, 1999, *Pollution Prevention and Abatement Handbook (Preliminary Version)*, available at *http://wbln0018.worldbank. org/essd/PMExt.nsf.*

Wheeler, D., 1997, "Information in Pollution Management: The New Model," in Von Amsberg (1997).

End Notes

1. For a comprehensive discussion of FEEMA's problems, see Von Amsberg (1996).

2. For further discussion of the new approach, see Hanrahan, Keene, Shaman, and Wheeler (1998) and World Bank (1999).

3. Interviews with staff members of CETESB and FEEMA.

4. For a detailed discussion of this issue, see Lovei (1995).

5. These cases are drawn from the authors' collaborative experience with environmental agencies in Colombia, Indonesia, and Philippines.

The New Model

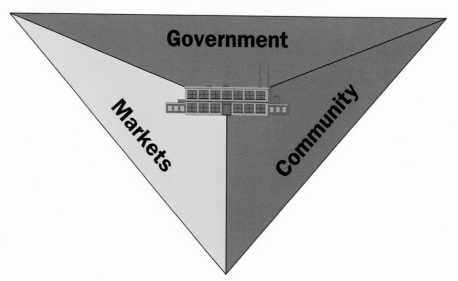

Government

Markets

Community

Chapter Seven

Greening Industry: The New Model

L ooking ahead with moderate optimism, we can imagine that the Earth's population has stabilized at 10 billion by the year 2050. About half the people live in today's developing countries, and a half century of 5 percent annual growth has given them incomes of $4,000 per capita—twice the level in middle-income countries at the turn of the century. People still aspire to higher incomes, but desperate poverty has been vanquished.

Who wouldn't welcome such a prospect? It could materialize, since many countries have achieved 5 percent growth since 1950. But a shadow looms when we realize that this scenario would entail a 25-fold growth in output and potentially huge increases in pollution. Reacting to such numbers, some people argue that the world's poor will never enjoy material prosperity because industrial civilization will run headlong into an environmental catastrophe.

The full story of environment and development has yet to be told, and we cannot guarantee a happy ending. Global warming, deforestation, loss of biodiversity, and other problems remain daunting. Our own work has focused on only one chapter of the story, and one basic question: Can societies hold local, not global, industrial pollution within acceptable bounds while industry continues to grow? For this question, at least, the answer appears to be yes—if we are clever and careful.

We are optimistic because greening industry is not a futurist fantasy. In every country, no matter how poor, some factories already operate at world-class environmental standards, and many profitable enterprises comply with national pollution regulations. Furthermore, extensive research has shown that sound, focused economic and environmental policies can greatly increase the number of good performers. Some of these measures entail reform of national economic policies, some require innovative and cost-effective approaches to formal regulation, and some harness the power of communities and markets to influence polluters through informal channels.

In this report, we have highlighted several innovative programs that demonstrate the potential for pollution reduction. Pilot projects are spreading as more countries decide to experiment with the new approaches, and broader experience will improve our understanding of their strengths and limitations. For the present, we can report that the results to date look promising. They suggest that coordinated action an all three fronts—economic reform, formal regulation, and informal regulation—can reduce industrial pollution significantly, even in very poor countries.

7.1 The Keys to Progress

Sustained progress on pollution control in developing countries depends on clear evidence that its benefits and costs compare favorably with those of other social investments. From Beijing to São Paulo, recent studies have verified that abatement of critical pollutants is a sound investment in many urban areas. However, regulating all pollutants under all conditions is neither economically defensible nor politically sustainable. Regulators have limited skills and resources, and they will rapidly lose political support if the public regards them as sloppy, unfair or ill informed. In Indonesia, the PROPER public disclosure program has demonstrated the impact of strategies that focus on accurately tracking and reporting a few critical pollutants from large emitters.

To maintain political support, environmental agencies need to marshal reliable information, educate the public about environmental tradeoffs, and encourage broad participation in setting goals. Such participation plays an important role in maintaining the credibility of Colombia's pollution charge system, EcoWatch in Philippines, and Indonesia's PROPER program. In PROPER, for example, stakeholders have an opportunity to vet the program's plant-level ratings before they are disclosed, forcing the agency to discipline its system for gathering, analyzing, and reporting data. And as the case of Ciudad Juárez in Mexico shows, communities that participate in regulation will support its objectives, provide information about local polluters, and defend the environmental agency against political attack.

FEEMA's sustained outreach efforts in Rio de Janeiro reveal that good relations with business leaders are crucial as well, since industry associations often have the political clout to veto pollution-control programs. Regulators will find natural allies among CEOs of firms whose market position depends on good environmental performance. Having already paid for cleaner production, these leaders will support measures that require similar efforts from their competitors.

Leveraging Polluters' Incentives

Finally and most critically, progress requires understanding that managers do not sanction pollution because they enjoy fouling the air and water, but because they are trying to minimize costs. At the factory level, the marginal expected penalty for polluting (MEP) tends to rise with emissions intensity. But when managers reduce emissions, they also increase the plant's marginal abatement cost (MAC)—the price of abating the next unit of pollution. So managers try to minimize their overall costs by adjusting emissions until MAC approximately equals MEP.

Governments have many opportunities to influence this plant-level balancing act by reducing MAC or raising MEP (Figure 7.1). Governments can reduce MAC through national reforms such as liberalizing trade, privatizing national industries, and promoting new stock markets. Research in China, India, Mexico, Indonesia, and other developing counties has demonstrated the power of such measures. But economic reform is no panacea, because some policies can produce perverse environmental impacts. In Ciudad Juárez, for example, Mexico's decision to end propane subsidies dealt a devastating blow to the local campaign for cleaner brick production. National economic reformers can contribute to the fight against pollution by anticipating such impacts and working with environmental agencies to counter them. Appropriate measures may include strengthening formal regulation in critically affected areas, supporting more public dissemination of environmental information, and slowing implementation of environmentally risky reforms while local environmental institutions adapt to the new demands. Coordinating economic reforms and environmental policies will require close contact between the relevant national ministries. A formally

Figure 7.1 Policy Options for Pollution Control

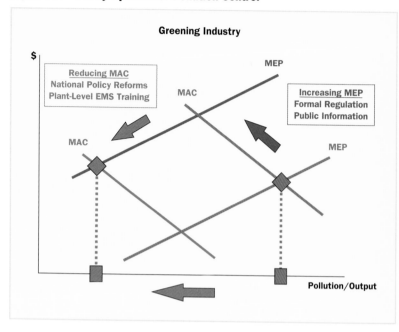

constituted environmental advisory unit for the key economics ministers may provide the best guarantee that economic reform programs will incorporate such concerns.

At the sectoral level, governments can lower MAC by supporting environmental management training for small and medium-size enterprises. The example of Guadalajara, Mexico, suggests that such programs can provide a cost-effective complement to conventional regulation. Documented experience remains limited, however. More studies of pilot programs are needed to assess the strengths and limitations of environmental management training under different developing-country conditions.

At the plant level, regulators can raise MEP through both formal and informal channels. Among formal instruments, market-based instruments such as pollution charges reduce emissions at the lowest cost because they leave abatement decisions in the hands of factory managers. Successful experiences in China, Colombia, and Philippines have shown that pollution charges are feasible and effective in developing countries. Tradable pollution permits may also work well, but successful developing-country experiences have not yet been documented. Although interest in market-based instruments is spreading, many regulators will continue to rely on standards-based regulation for some time. Even so, targeted programs like São Paulo's ABC approach have demonstrated that traditional regulation can be reasonably cost-effective if monitoring and enforcement are focused on large pollution sources with low abatement costs.

Regulators can encourage informal regulation by publishing reliable, easily understood information on pollution sources and their impacts. Both EcoWatch in Philippines and PROPER in Indonesia have shown that public disclosure can have a strong impact even where formal regulation is weak, because it enlists social norms and market forces in pressuring polluters to clean up. Public information programs carry the extra benefit of generating political support for pollution control, by educating communities and raising the credibility of environmental agencies.

7.2 The New Model for Controlling Pollution

The proliferation of these new formal and informal channels is effectively creating a new model for pollution control (Figure 7.2). In this model, regulation is much more information intensive and transparent. As an environmental agency exerts influence through numerous channels, it becomes more like a mediator and less like a

Figure 7.2 New Dimensions for Policy

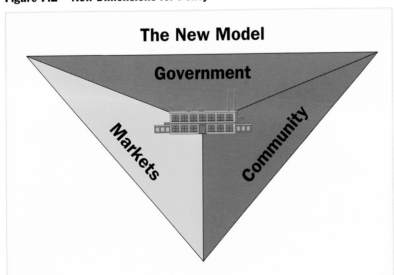

dictator. Community representatives take their place at the negotiating table along with regulators and factory managers. Market agents make their presence felt as well, through decisions by consumers, bankers, and stockholders.

The new model empowers policymakers because it gives them many options for improving industry's environmental performance. But the model also imposes new responsibilities—for strategic thinking about the benefits and costs of pollution control; a strong commitment to public education and participation; intelligent, focused use of information technology; and a willingness to adopt new approaches such as pollution charges and public disclosure. Of course, regulators will always have important responsibilities for traditional monitoring and enforcement. But in the future they will use more of their resources to raise MEP through informal regulation, to lower MAC through support for improved environmental management by small firms, and to promote sustainable economic reforms by working more closely with national policymakers.

The new approach pays particular attention to the problems of the poor. Recent research has shown that pollution intensity declines steadily as per capita income rises, both within and across countries. But economic development takes a long time, and the poor suffer heavily from pollution now. Evidence from Mexico, China, and elsewhere has shown that education provides a powerful lever for near-term improvement: Even if people are poor, they will not passively accept pollution if they are well informed about its sources and impacts. Through public education and maintenance of appropriate environmental standards, governments can help assure basic amenities and human dignity for the poor during the transition to greener industry.

7.3 The Role of the World Bank

The World Bank makes significant contributions to controlling industrial pollution on several fronts. By encouraging nations to adopt needed economic reforms, it influences pollution's "hidden half." In the long run, support for growth-oriented policies will encourage stricter pollution control by more prosperous societies. But the Bank has learned that not all economic reforms have clean impacts in the near term. It has recently revised its operational guidelines to ensure that Bank-supported reform programs incorporate environmental concerns. Successfully implementing these guidelines will require sustained effort, coordination between the Bank's economists and environmental specialists, and active collaboration between economic ministries and environmental agencies in partner countries.

The Bank has also financed decentralized environmental information systems that support the new regulatory model. Here the emphasis should be on appropriate scale, since experience cautions against using the most sophisticated modeling and data-processing technology to address all possible environmental problems. This comprehensive approach, which could be encouraged by the Bank's preference for big loans, can easily distract regulators from confronting their communities' most critical pollution problems. And once regulators have lost focus and clarity of purpose, their performance and credibility soon dwindle as well.

For several years, the Bank has catalyzed new thinking on pollution regulation by supporting pilot projects and disseminating their lessons to the international community. Partner environmental agencies have taken the lead, but the Bank has provided technical assistance, financial backing, and public support for innovative ideas. Recent initiatives of this kind include the Guadalajara small business assistance project in Mexico, the pollution charge programs in Philippines and Colombia, state-level environmental management reforms in Brazil, and public disclosure programs in Indonesia, Philippines, Mexico, and Colombia.

How can the World Bank promote the new model in the coming decade? Critical tasks include continued sponsorship of innovative pilot projects, widespread dissemination of their results, development of environmental loans that expand successful pilots to large-scale programs, and serious incorporation of environmental concerns into loans that support national economic reforms.

The Bank can use several instruments to support pilot projects, including the new Learning and Innovation Loans, Bank-administered environmental trust funds, and support of technical assistance as a "nonlending service" by the Bank's country operations units. The World Bank Institute should play the lead role in disseminating new ideas, through its international policy seminars and training programs for environmental professionals.

The Bank can expand pilot projects to large-scale programs through loans for development of pollution management systems that embody key principles of the new approach: focus, transparency, community participation, and regulatory instruments that leverage the economic incentives faced by polluters. To be successful, these operations should promote a clear view of environmental objectives, cost-effective instruments for achieving those objectives, efficient gathering and analysis of appropriate environmental information, and, certainly not least, a strong capacity to enforce regulations when necessary.

Although the Bank also provides direct financing for pollution control, it has learned that subsidizing abatement investments by large, individual polluters is seldom the best way to control air and water emissions. Such polluters will generally mobilize their own resources to abate pollution if regulators properly leverage MAC and MEP. The major exception is construction of sewerage facilities: Household sewage remains a prime source of health damage in most poor countries, and the Bank provides support when communities cannot issue their own bonds to finance municipal sewerage and wastewater treatment systems. Further research will be needed to determine whether, and under what conditions, the Bank and other lending institutions should also finance common treatment facilities for industrial development parks and other areas where factories cluster.

The Bank can also promote the new approach through its lending operations that support national economic reforms. These operations provide an excellent opportunity for strengthening environmental agencies' ability to measure changes in environmental quality, identify serious pollution sources, and employ formal and informal regulatory instruments to counter excessive emissions. They can also promote the development of new links between economic and environmental ministries, thereby increasing the capacity of partner countries to cope with the environmental consequences of future economic changes.

In summary, the coming decade will offer the World Bank many opportunities to assist its partner countries in controlling industrial pollution while working to eliminate poverty. The Bank can promote the new model by encouraging innovative experiments, disseminating their results, expanding the success stories to national programs, and ensuring that economic reform programs incorporate environmental concerns. Through all of these channels, the Bank's activities can hasten the greening of industry in many poor countries.